CREATING
Q*BERT

and Other Classic Video Arcade Games

by **WARREN DAVIS**

Foreword by **ED BOON**

Afterword by **JOHN NEWCOMER**

SANTA MONICA PRESS

Published by:
Santa Monica Press LLC
P.O. Box 850
Solana Beach, CA 92075
1-800-784-9553
www.santamonicapress.com
books@santamonicapress.com

Printed in the United States

Santa Monica Press books are available at special quantity discounts when purchased in bulk by corporations, organizations, or groups. Please call our Special Sales department at 1-800-784-9553.

This book is intended to provide general information. The publisher, author, distributor, and copyright owner are not engaged in rendering professional advice or services. The publisher, author, distributor, and copyright owner are not liable or responsible to any person or group with respect to any loss, illness, or injury caused or alleged to be caused by the information found in this book.

ISBN-13 978-1-59580-105-0

Publisher's Cataloging-in-Publication data

Names: Davis, Warren B., 1956-, author. | Boon, Ed, foreword author. | Newcomer, John, afterword author.
Title: Creating Q*bert and other classic video arcade games / by Warren Davis; foreword by Ed Boon; afterword by John Newcomer.
Description: Solana Beach, CA: Santa Monica Press, 2021.
Identifiers: ISBN: 978-1-59580-105-0 (paperback) | 978-1-59580-785-4 (ebook)
Subjects: LCSH Davis, Warren B., 1956- | Video game designers--Biography. | Computer programmers--Biography. | Video games--Design--History. | Electronic games--Design--History. | BISAC BIOGRAPHY & AUTOBIOGRAPHY / Personal Memoirs | BIOGRAPHY & AUTOBIOGRAPHY / Entertainment & Performing Arts | GAMES AND ACTIVITIES / Video & Mobile | COMPUTERS / Programming / Games | COMPUTERS / Design, Graphics & Media / Video & Animation
Classification: LCC GV1469.3 .D38 2021 | DDC 794.8/092--dc23

Cover and interior design and production by Future Studio

Dedicated to
Ron Waxman and Howie Rubin

CONTENTS

FOREWORD

by Ed Boon
Co-creator of *Mortal Kombat* and
NetherRealm Studios creative director

Like many teenagers in the '80s, I was drawn into the world of video games. I not only loved playing them, but was obsessed with how they were made. That obsession drew me into computer programming and eventually I found myself working at Williams Electronics in October of 1986. Even though I was hired to program pinball machines, they put me in a dark section of the video game department referred to as the "Dead Zone." This is where I met Warren Davis, whose cubicle was directly across from my office. Warren already had a number of games under his belt, including the classic game *Q*bert*. I soon learned Warren was one of a number of industry veterans I was working with, many of whom created some of my favorite games like *Defender*, *Robotron*, and *Joust*.

At Williams Electronics, Warren was working on multiple projects, including *Joust 2*, *Lotto Fun* (a video lottery game), and software tools to help artists work more efficiently. After learning who he was, I remember nagging Warren for details about how *Q*bert* was created but he was usually too busy to dive deep into that story. You can imagine how excited I was to read this book!

Today I think of Warren as both a celebrated and unsung hero at the same time. While he is certainly known as "The *Q*bert* Guy," I feel his work at Williams/Midway made an even bigger impact on the game industry. It's just that fewer people know this.

During my three years in the pinball group, Warren was part of a small team building Williams' next generation of video arcade hardware and software. By the time I joined the video game department, they had built a development foundation upon which future classic arcade games like *NARC, Smash TV, Terminator 2, NBA Jam,* and *Mortal Kombat* would be created.

What gave Williams/Midway games a competitive edge was their digitized graphics, which were created by converting video of real-world objects to game graphics. The result was a photo-realistic look that no other game company could touch. However, the process of digitizing game graphics was very time consuming for video artists. Warren wrote groundbreaking software tools that automated that digitizing process, animated our sprites, compressed our images, managed our color palettes, and probably more than I can remember. These utilities sped up our workflow exponentially. I can't overstate the impact Warren had on the development of *Mortal Kombat* and so many other Williams/Midway games.

As you might imagine, someone who created *Q*bert* and helped build the foundation for the Williams/ Midway games probably has a lot of fascinating stories to tell. This book is a great collection of those stories. There is a genuine honesty here that covers not only the successes, but also the disappointments, disagreements, and flat-out arguments involved in making so many classic games. I loved reading not only how *Q*bert* was created, but also Warren's perspective on cancelled projects, office politics, as well as his departure and return to Williams/Midway.

I'm writing this as one of many game makers who were not only inspired by Warren's games, but also benefitted immensely from the software tools he created. I

had a great time reading this book, and particularly enjoyed Warren's (almost perfect) recollection of the early
days in the Williams "Dead Zone" offices. Warren remembered who occupied every workspace! Except two,
admitting "...but I have no recollection of who were in the
other two." For the record, I was one of the forgotten two.
But hey, it's been 35 years! ☺

INTRODUCTION

Throughout my career, many people have asked me: "How do you become a video game creator?" My answer to that question has changed gradually over the years. At the moment, it's "I haven't the faintest idea."

The industry is so radically different from when I entered it way back in the prehistoric time of January 1982. Now there are so many areas of specialization: game designers, engine designers, engine programmers, effects programmers, scripters, A.I. programmers, U.I. programmers, U.I. designers, level designers, character animators, background animators, producers, asset managers, testers. Not to mention lighting designers, sound designers, voice and motion capture actors, and a whole slew of other types of people who all play a part in the creation of a video game.

When I started, if you wanted to create a game, you were one of three things: a programmer, an artist, or a sound designer. No one was just a game designer—you had to have at least one other useful skill. Sure, there were other important tasks, hardware design most critically. But as far as the creative team went, that was it. For myself, having no knowledge of sound design whatsoever, only a minimal ability as an artist, and a degree in computer engineering, my choices were limited. I did some hardware design work after college, but my love of computers always revolved around programming. To me, programming a computer was a means of artistic expression. People's responses to a computer program mimic their responses to art. It can inspire anger or frustration when it misbehaves. It can make you smile if the program's creator has added a little levity into it. And there's a satisfaction to be had when it does exactly what you wanted it to do.

More importantly, after my earliest exposure to computers in high school, I realized they had a potential to entertain. And I found it pretty satisfying when I could use them for that purpose. I wasn't exactly the class clown as a kid, but I loved to laugh and make other people laugh. I didn't see myself as a performer, though—I lacked the confidence to get up on a stage in front of people (although that changed somewhat in college and ironically set me on a road to becoming an actor as well as a video game designer). I guess the thing that defined my motivation in career choices was that, above all, I loved the idea of being an "entertainer" in whatever form I could.

So when the first video arcade games showed up in the game room of my student union at the college where I was studying computer engineering, I was thrilled to discover that the very technology I had chosen for a career path could be capable of something so . . . entertaining! I dreamed of someday working on video games in any capacity, but it never occurred to me that I'd ever get that opportunity. I figured you had to be special, be a genius, know the right people—qualities which all seemed out of my grasp. I didn't realize that a lot of it has to do with being in the right place at the right time. Which, as I'll explain later, is where I found myself in the cold Chicago winter of 1981. Dumb luck, really.

Many years later, when arcades were on the wane and home system graphics were becoming more advanced—when memory was cheaper and processors were faster and the types of games we could only imagine in 1982 were becoming reality—I could never have guessed there would be a resurgence of interest in those old, seemingly crude games. I posted my first online recollections about the development of *Q*bert* sometime in the mid-1990s at the request of a fan who contacted me. The internet was still a pretty new thing at the time, especially to me. In 1999, I attended my first Classic Gaming Expo in Las Vegas as a panelist and guest. I think it'd be accurate to say I was astonished that people cared so much about work I'd done almost twenty years earlier.

I started to get a small amount of attention as a "classic game designer," which, although rewarding, certainly did not go to my head. Even now, when people I'm around learn that I designed and programmed *Q*bert*, the reactions I get are one of the following:

1) OH MY GOD! YOU MADE *Q*BERT*!
    I LOVE THAT GAME!
2) Oh, that's nice.
3) What's *Q*bert*?

The first answer is of course very gratifying. I think there are few pleasures in life that can compete with having done something that has touched people's lives in a positive way. And believe me, I'm well aware that my contribution to human existence, such as it is, is somewhat slight. Let's face it, I haven't cured cancer or improved any of society's ills. But enough people have expressed their fondness for *Q*bert* that I can't help but be truly touched and grateful. The second and third answers are more of what I expect, though, and they keep my ego in check.

So this growing phenomenon of retro-gaming nostalgia provided me with opportunities to tell some stories and share experiences through magazine articles and appearances at comic-cons and retro-gaming events. And I began to realize just how many stories there were to tell, how many experiences I've had thanks to being in the right place at the right time that might actually be of interest to others. If I'm known at all, it's for my work on *Q*bert*, but most people don't know anything about a LaserDisc game I made called *Us vs. Them*, which to me is a much more fascinating story. Or my involvement in the creation of *Mortal Kombat* and *NBA Jam* through the system I developed to digitize live actors into a video game. Or the time I spent with Aerosmith during the making of *Revolution X*.

So many stories. And so many other people involved.

Most of my time in the arcade industry was divided between just two companies: Gottlieb and Williams. There were many people I worked with at those companies who have stories that may be equally as—or more fascinating than—mine. There were also other companies—Stern, Cinematronics, Atari, Bally/Midway, and Incredible Technologies, to name just a few—each with their own stories, no doubt. But I hadn't seen anyone else collecting their stories into a book, and it seemed a shame if someone didn't start the ball rolling. None of us are getting any younger and once we're gone, many of those untold stories will be, too. There have been some documentaries about the early days of video games and plenty of books, but when I started writing up my stories, none had been written firsthand by the people who were there. (Thankfully, that's no longer true. A few firsthand accounts have since been published.) Also, I can't tell you how many times I've seen articles about some facet of the industry that I was involved in where the facts are, to some degree, wrong. For an example, just go to the *Q*bert* page on Wikipedia and look at the discussion tab.

I wasn't one of the original pioneers of video games. I came into the industry at the tail end of what could be called its "golden age," and I benefited from the breakthroughs of those that came before me. But video games were still new. Boundaries were being pushed and the lexicon was still evolving. I witnessed a lot and contributed a bit.

Because I was lucky enough to be there during those early days of the video game industry—a time of exploration and uncertainty, of pushing the envelope of a new technology, of creating the building blocks of a new art form—I've decided to share what it was like. For me, at least.

I want to stress that this isn't intended as a history book, although it certainly covers some history and who knows, maybe someday the stories within these pages may be considered as having some historical significance. That's not up to me, it's up to the historians of the future. My desire in writing this book is to share my journey and my perceptions of the events that happened to me and around me.

While many memories have been jogged by recent conversations with old colleagues, let me be clear that these are strictly *my* memories, unless otherwise indicated. I recently met up with one particular colleague at Gallifrey One, the annual *Doctor Who* convention here in Los Angeles. He was a fellow programmer at Williams/Bally/Midway back in the day, and we got to talking about this book. I mentioned that there really aren't any villains in my stories. Not that it was all love and sunshine; there were moments of tension, anger, and bitterness among people at times. But even as I wrote about those types of incidents in my career, I recall no lasting animosities. Somehow, his experiences were a bit different. He remembered a lot of feuds, arguments, and downright nasty behavior that I've either forgotten or just wasn't present to see. Maybe his memoir would be a more interesting read, but my perspective is the one I've shared here.

So while I've tried to ensure the accuracy of my memories through conversations with others who were there, slight errors of detail may have emerged, and for that I apologize. That's on me. But as I said, this isn't intended to be a history book. Hopefully through my recollections, you'll be able feel some of what I felt—the joy, the disappointment, the wonder, the frustration, and the satisfaction.

And above all, I hope you'll be entertained.

Warren Davis

CHAPTER ONE

THE SHAPING OF A YOUNG MIND

It's hard to believe now, entering the third decade of the twenty-first century, that there ever was a time without video games. They've become a standard part of most childhoods, and have evolved as both a business and an art form. There can be complexity in the storytelling, beauty in the visuals, and nuance in the aural. They can achieve startling levels of realism that mimic the world we live in, or they can create fantastic never-before-seen worlds with astounding believability. And they require the player to participate.

It wasn't always this way. When I was a kid, my primary form of entertainment was television. We didn't even have a color TV, not that it mattered since many shows were filmed in black and white. There was no such thing as a VCR then, so after a program aired, that was it. If you missed it, you missed it. The only way you could see it again was if they re-ran it in the summer. Sounds rough, I know. Yet my parents were fond of reminding me that they grew up in a time when even television didn't exist. All they had was radio.

The drawback of both television and radio is that they are non-interactive media. Sure, you can laugh or cry or yell at it, but you can't affect what you're seeing or hearing. The true breakthrough of the video game as entertainment is that you can. You do. Generally, you must.

Or you might as well be watching TV. The astonishing technology that allowed for this breakthrough was the computer.

From the time I was born through my early childhood, computers were the size of rooms. When you saw them on TV or in movies, they generally had a lot of blinking lights and spinning tape drives, maybe an oscilloscope with some wavy lines on it, and a teletype machine for printouts. In science fiction programs, they might look bizarre and futuristic. Often they could talk to you and had personalities. The notion that this might be at all possible was amazing and made me want to learn more about these real-but-somewhat-mystical devices. I was so enthralled that when I was a young teen, I went out and bought a "build your own computer" kit. It was made out of plastic mostly and metal rods, and wasn't much more than a mechanical adding machine. But no matter—I was fascinated! It seemed amazing that just by pulling on some levers, a bunch of mechanical parts would move around, and suddenly I'd get answers to basic arithmetic problems.

"How did it know?" I wondered. I had built the thing, and I still couldn't fathom it. Of course, it didn't have much of a personality or talk to me, but it made me want to learn more.

HIGH SCHOOL

I was encouraged to pursue my curiosity about computers while attending Sheepshead Bay High School in Brooklyn, New York. It was the fall of 1970 when I started the tenth grade, and to my surprise and joy, there was a computer lab (pretty rare for a high school in those days).

I started hanging around the computer room and

became friends with the guys who were in charge, Arthur Apter and Kenny Ross, who were both seniors during my sophomore year. Arthur was, well, let's face it, a nerdy guy, almost a stereotype of a nerd. But he was very generous with his time and knowledge, and took me under his wing. He also had a wicked sense of humor. Kenny was a big, jovial guy who provided a stark physical contrast to Arthur, and also had a great sense of humor. I loved watching these two interact. They'd talk about something, disagree, then argue, sometimes viciously, and finally come to agreement. The next year, they both started at MIT and I took a trip to Cambridge, Massachusetts, to visit them. It was my first trip away from New York by myself. Hijinks ensued. Being around them was pretty fun and stimulating.

For some reason, during their senior year Arthur and Kenny never found a junior to take charge of the SBHS computer after they graduated. So I became their replacement. Trouble was, as a sophomore, I hadn't been allowed to take the computer math class that was a prerequisite for the job. Not only that, the teacher who'd been teaching the computer class was leaving, and the school had to train someone else to do it. The solution was for me and the new computer math teacher to learn the particulars about our computer at the same time, during the summer between my tenth and eleventh grades. The sweetest part of this arrangement was that the new computer math teacher turned out to be the lovely Miss Seiderman, my geometry teacher from tenth grade who I had a major crush on. It wasn't just that she had the physical beauty of a magazine model; she also had a smile that reached into your soul and a laugh that warmed you like a fire. Needless to say, I had a great time that summer. Learning computers and being near the blonde goddess of my dreams one-on-one.

In the fall, Miss Seiderman began teaching computer math, and I took the class even though I'd learned the material along with her during the summer. I didn't mind . . . it meant more time around her. And I became something of a secret weapon for her. There were times when she'd tell the class something, and if she wasn't sure she was getting it right, she'd look over at me and I'd subtly nod, or shake my head to help her along.

The computer at the center of all this was called the Monrobot XI, made by Monroe Business Machines. I'm not sure how long it had been there—certainly for a few years before I arrived. I have a vague recollection of hearing that it was a hand-me-down from its original owner. This particular machine wasn't the size of a room, but the size of a desk. Actually, it *was* a desk, on the outside at least. Its claim to fame was an appearance on the TV show *I Dream of Jeannie*. In the two-episode story "The Girl Who Never Had a Birthday," directed by Claudio Guzman and written by Sidney Sheldon, the character Tony (played by Larry Hagman) uses a computer named ERIC to find Jeannie's birthday. He goes into a room filled with—you guessed it—closet-sized cabinets with blinking lights and spinning tape reels, and in the center of the room is an L-shaped desk with a typewriter on top . . . the Monrobot XI!

The typewriter was the main input-output device. CRT (Cathode Ray Tube) computer monitors—essentially old-style TVs with slightly different electronics to process a signal from a computer rather than a TV tuner—were not yet common, although within a few years they would be. Of course, in today's world, they've been replaced with flat-screen technologies. But in 1971, we had a typewriter. You typed your input, and the computer typed its responses. Where the left desk drawer would normally go, there was a paper tape reader and punch,

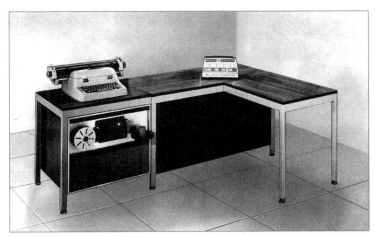

The Monrobot XI Computer.

used to save and load programs. Although it was called "tape," the paper tape wasn't sticky. It was just paper, about an inch wide, but it came wound onto reels, much like reel-to-reel recording tape. There was room for up to eight holes to be punched across the width of the tape. Since there are 8 bits in a byte of computer memory, every line of holes represented 1 byte.

You'd type in a program on the typewriter and get it working, and then to save it (which you had to do because the Monrobot XI had little to no non-volatile memory), the computer punched your program onto a strip of paper tape, which you'd then rip off and save. The longer the program, the longer the tape. Once you had your paper tape, you could load it back into the computer without typing. The Monrobot XI's memory capacity was 1,024 words (32 bits each) or 4 kilobytes total. Programs had to be written in the computer's assembly language, essentially a numeric language that's ultimately all that any computer understands. Consequently, learning to program a computer back then wasn't for everyone. Along with being good at math and logic, you had to have a real desire, because entering and debugging programs could be a frustrating task.

If you look back at the history of computing, I think you'll find that even in the earliest days, people found ways to use computers for games. The Monrobot XI was no exception, despite having no CRT screen. One of its best games was a horse racing simulation. It credited you with some "money," then showed you a list of horses and their odds. You placed bets and then, using only the typewriter and the paper tape punch to make sound effects, the computer ran the race. It was pretty exciting. After the race ended, the money got tallied up, and you could race some more. One of the most ingenious parts of this program was that at the start of each race, it used the paper tape punch to sound like the bugle call you'd hear at the start of a real horse race.

Our computer lab at SBHS also had a punch card machine. It was made by a company called Dura, and that's what we called it—The Dura. One morning, Miss Seiderman came into the computer room and found a note I'd left her after staying late the previous day. It said: "There's a bug in the Dura!!" She freaked out, thinking that somehow the machine was broken. It, too, was a hand-me-down and I don't think we had any budget to repair it. It wasn't until later in the day that I got to explain—when I had been using it the previous day, I'd seen an actual insect crawling around under the keys.

You may be wondering . . . what the heck is a punch card machine? Well, back in the olden times there were these things called punch cards. Each card was made from heavy paper stock and measured $7\frac{3}{8}$ by $3\frac{1}{4}$ inches. One card could hold up to eighty characters and represented one line of a computer program. You'd type each line of your program into a punch card machine (i.e., The Dura), which would encode each character by punching tiny rectangular holes in the card. When you were done, your program was a stack of punched cards.

But our Monrobot XI didn't take punch cards as input. The reason we had a punch card machine at SBHS was that we had an agreement with Brooklyn College allowing us to run programs on their mainframe computer. These programs were written in a computer language called FORTRAN that was considered higher-level than assembly language because it more resembled English. (Barely. But it did use keywords like Read, Write, Print, Do, If, Then, etc.) A single line of FORTRAN might represent a handful of assembly language statements.

Normally, once your program was "punched" into a deck, you'd walk it over to the computer mainframe and drop it off. Since we were in high school, all of our programs were collected and driven over to Brooklyn College's computer lab. Later, a computer operator would place your stack of cards into a machine that read your program—not unlike, in principle, how the paper tape reader of the Monrobot XI would read paper tapes. The computer would run your program and generate a printout with the results. Then, that printout and your cards would be left for you to pick up. Turnaround times could vary based on how many students needed to run programs, but twenty-four hours was not uncommon.

So, what if your program had a bug? Well, you had to examine the printout, find the bug, then re-punch the lines that needed to change, insert the corrected cards back into the deck properly, and go through the process again.

If this system seems like the equivalent of rubbing two sticks together to start a fire, you're absolutely right. You could carry smaller stacks of cards wrapped in rubber bands, but large programs were so big and weighed so much, you had to carry them around in boxes. Keeping the cards in order was also of paramount importance. God help you if you dropped your box and the cards spilled out. I saw it happen more than once when I was in college. It was as if you'd handwritten a novel and the wind blew your pages all over the place.

Once, our computer class took a field trip to Brooklyn College to visit their computer lab, so we could see what was happening to our programs between handing off the cards and getting back a printout. We got to go beyond the exterior desk where students handed in their decks of punch cards, into a climate-controlled, fluorescent-lit room where the floor was about a foot above the actual floor, so cables could be routed underneath. The room was filled with many large cabinets of mysterious electronics and an industrial-size printer noisily spewing out a continuous stream of program results.

Still, the trip wasn't that interesting. Sure, the computer was big and the whole sterile vibe of the place was a big change from our high school lab, which was basically a classroom with the Monrobot XI and Dura off to the side. But then we got to see something really special. Our guide took us to a room that had an oscilloscope, which is basically a type of vector-based CRT designed to display waveforms and measure voltages and other boring stuff. The screen was circular and small and in the center was a tiny line drawing of what looked like the Starship *Enterprise* flying past jagged, rock-like floating line images. A joystick allowed you to rotate the ship and fire dot-sized photon torpedoes that broke the rocks into smaller rocks upon contact. If a rock slammed into the *Enterprise*, the lines that made up the ship would break apart and spin off in different directions.

I'd never seen anything like this. I wasn't aware of it at the time, but it turns out that some form of this game had been passed around since the 1960s among owners of early PDP minicomputers, which many colleges had. My mind was blown!

Inspired by this and the horse racing game, I began to look for ways to have some fun and give my Monrobot some personality. One program I wrote was an implementation of Mad Libs. The computer asked for different types of words: noun, verb, adjective, name, place, etc. After you typed in whatever random choices came to mind, it used those to fill in the blanks of a pre-programmed template and type out what turned out to be a ridiculous-sounding story.

Another program I wrote purported to be a simple calculator. It asked you for numbers to perform an operation on, but would randomly give back some attitude. If you were to look at the typewriter output from a session, it might look something like this.

(Stuff shown on the left is typed by the computer. Stuff shown on the right is typed by the user.)

Enter number: 324
Enter second number: 42
Enter operation (+,-,/,*)   /
The answer is 7.7142857142857

Enter number: 165
Enter second number: 213
Enter operation (+,-,/,*)   *

I'm sorry, I don't like those numbers. Try again.

Enter number: 165
Enter second number: 213
Enter operation (+,-,/,*)   *

Hey, are you deaf? I said try something else!

```
Enter number:            741
Enter second number:     629
Enter operation (+,-,/,*)  +
```

You know, I'm kinda tired. Come back later.
Zzzzzzzzzzzzzzzzzzzzzzzzz . . . . .

You get the idea. Childish? You bet. But then again, I was pretty much a child. And I thought this was just a hoot. I loved watching people's faces when they encountered this, because they never saw it coming. It was outside of the realm of their experience with computers. People expected computers to be dry, unfunny things. They didn't necessarily realize that behind every computer program is a human being telling the computer what to do.

My high school years had a mildly amusing end. And while this story has nothing to do with video games, I can't think of another opportunity to tell it, so here it is.

I was chosen to receive the Math award at graduation. An honor, to be sure. But two days before the ceremony, I sprained my ankle playing basketball and it swelled up to the size of a baseball. I could barely walk! I wanted to skip the ceremony altogether, but my parents wouldn't let me. So I had to hobble to graduation on crutches. My graduating class had something like 900 students, and the school rented out a large movie theater in Brooklyn to accommodate everyone. When I got to the theater, I learned that the students getting awards were supposed to march up onto the stage and sit there throughout the ceremony. The rest of the students would sit in the first rows of the audience, with family and friends behind them. All students, both in the audience and onstage, would be separated by gender, with the boys wearing royal-blue caps and gowns and entering from the right while the girls, wearing white, entered from the left. Since I couldn't walk, they pre-sat me on the boys' side of the stage before the whole thing started.

So there I was, sitting alone onstage in this huge theater, patiently waiting for things to start. Now that I think about it, it's possible that this experience helped cure me of my distaste with being in front of large groups. No matter how uncomfortable I was being absolutely alone onstage, I wasn't ambulatory enough to do anything about it, so I had no choice but to get used to it.

Finally, after what seemed an eternity, the ceremony began. The graduating class entered from the back of the theater and filed in through the aisles. Most took their seats in the front rows, while the girls and boys receiving awards continued onto the stage from the left and right sides respectively. But then, unexpectedly, the boys continued moving past me and criss-crossed with the girls, who were now heading directly towards me. Yes, that's right. For some unknown reason, I'd been placed on the girls' side of the stage—a royal-blue raisin in a sea of white gowns.

When it came time to get my award, the presenter called my name and turned toward the boys' side, confused that no one was getting up. I stood up, supporting myself with one crutch and waving the other one in the air, yelling, "Over here!" The crowd reacted with a huge laugh. With that, the seeds were planted for my future acting career.

COLLEGE

I became a college freshman at Rensselaer Polytechnic Institute in the fall of 1973, a year notable for a number of technological happenings. The bank on campus installed a newfangled device called an Automated Teller Machine. Texas Instruments released their first handheld electronic calculator, the SR-10, replacing the ubiquitous slide rule that had hung on the belt of every engineering student for generations. And I saw a video arcade game for the first time ever.

RPI's Student Union had a game room that took up the entire length of the south side of the building's lowest level. As you entered, you could see bowling lanes on your left, ping-pong and pool tables on your right, and a desk in front of you where you traded your ID for bowling shoes, a ping-pong paddle, or a pool cue. What you couldn't immediately see was the smallish room behind that desk. The arcade. An arcade in those days meant mostly pinball machines and some other electro-mechanical coin-operated games, such as a baseball simulator or shuffle alley. (A shuffle alley is the arcade version of a bowling machine. You push a metal puck down a flat playfield. It slides under a set of plastic "pins" and over metal switches that determine which "pins" get eliminated.) These games were "electro-mechanical" in that they had some simple electronics inside which responded to mechanical parts that the player interacted with.

At some point during my freshman year, a couple of burly maintenance men wheeled what looked like a refrigerator box into the arcade. Inside that big box was a machine that was heavy on the electronics but light on the mechanical. No one I knew had ever seen anything like it before. It was a video game—*Pong*, to be precise. As it was unpacked, onlookers gathered in wonder. There was a large, upright cabinet that housed a TV, with a waist-high panel holding some buttons and knobs. It also had a coin box, just like on the pinball machines.

The machine seemed simple and bare. The screen was black and pretty much all it displayed were white dots. But it was an instant sensation, because it was interactive in a way most people had never experienced with a TV. I'd seen something like it on my trip to Brooklyn College when I was in high school, but this wasn't hidden in some computer lab. It was public. It was accessible. And it was instantly popular.

Pong was soon followed by other games such as *Tank*, *Breakout*, *Nibbler*, *Asteroids*, and more. There wasn't enough real estate to keep all the pinball machines, and their numbers dwindled. Eventually, some of the ping-pong and pool tables had to go to make room for these quarter-suckers. The video game revolution had begun.

GAME ON

In 1973, RPI had no computers with CRTs. Punch cards were still the primary way students communicated with the school's computer. CRT terminals that connected students to the mainframe didn't appear until sometime during my senior year. To put this in perspective, the Apple II wouldn't be introduced until I graduated in 1977. And the IBM PC, with its monochrome text-only display, came out in 1981. So this was still a formative time for computer graphics.

Despite having no graphical device to play with, I was lucky enough to find a way to inject game-play into my computer studies. RPI had a new experimental schedule that included a J-term (short for January Term). This was a month long semester in which students would take one class—usually something that wasn't part of their regular curriculum—to explore a topic of interest to them. I chose a class called Computers and Games. Since the only computer at my disposal was the school's mainframe, and the only input device available to me was a punch card reader, I thought it'd make sense to embrace the card concept. I chose as my class project to write a gin rummy simulator in FORTRAN.

I created fifty-two punch cards to represent a deck of playing cards, which I'd shuffle manually. Then I'd stick them at the end of my program and drop them off at the computer center. As my program ran, it would simulate a game between two players using the shuffled punch cards as the deck. The computer played both sides, taking turns and making decisions for each player until there was a winner. The printout I got back showed exactly what happened at each step of the simulation. It wasn't in any way an interactive experience, but by analyzing the printouts, I was able to find bugs and fix logic errors. Eventually the program was playing complete games in which each "player's" choices were as good as any human's.

Of course, gin rummy isn't as complicated as chess (which at the time was something of a Holy Grail for computer programmers to simulate), but it was challenging enough for a one-month class. And the best part was I could indulge my love of using computers for entertainment. In fact, my enjoyment of that J-term is solid proof of my dedication to using computers for games, given the absurd weight of the punch cards I had to lug around on an almost daily basis and the fact that Troy, New York, tends to be cold and covered in snow all through January. Few of my academic experiences at college were as enjoyable as this.

One exception was the following year's J-term. I took a class where we were supposedly exploring the use of computer graphics in making art. We had a black-and-white video camera connected to a color TV monitor through a circuit board that converted gray values into colors. Through a variety of knobs, you could control which colors different grays were mapped into, giving you some psychedelic video effects. Mind you, we weren't exploring the technology part of this. That was already done. We were just exploring the artistic possibilities—with a lovely female nude model! The camera was pointed at her as she'd move and dance, while we took turns fiddling with knobs and making her turn all sorts of crazy colors. I don't know how the professor talked the engineering department into funding this, but no one in the class was complaining. Actually, now that I think about it, I'm pretty sure the professor was the *head* of the engineering department.

As my college years continued, video arcade games became more widespread and varied. Occasionally, I thought about how cool it would be to create them, but I couldn't see myself in that role. A major reason for this was that I had absolutely no experience in programming graphics on a video monitor. And RPI, strangely behind the times on this new technology, had few opportunities to offer me.

My undergrad degree was called Computer and Systems Engineering, being a sort of newfangled hybrid between Computer Science (traditionally part of the Math Department) and Electrical Engineering (part of the Engineering Department). The notion of combining both hardware and software into a single program was a recent one, and RPI was just coming around to exploring it. This was unfortunate for me, since my goal was to somehow straddle both disciplines, and much of my undergraduate education in computer design was sadly theoretical. There weren't any courses where you actually got to build parts of a computer.

It was always expected (by my parents, though I had no objection) that I would stay on at RPI and get a master's degree. I'd been aware that RPI was doing some research on a Mars rover, and during my senior year I found out there was a segment of that research in which some data needed to be displayed graphically. Part of the requirement for a master's degree was a thesis project, so I excitedly committed to jumping on board this research team at the start of my fifth year.

When fall came around and I showed up to my first group meeting with the team, I quickly realized two things. First, the development of the graphical display had already been done, and second, the professor leading the project was a dictatorial tyrant. As I'm generally a person with somewhat healthy self-esteem, things did not go well between us. I wasn't happy with what I considered to be a bait and switch—the research I was expected to perform was highly theoretical and mathematical, having nothing to do with developing a graphical display—and I was not afraid to stand up to the professor's verbal abuse. I found myself dropping out of the master's program after one month.

This was the first huge decision I ever made in my life, and before making it I was terrified. For one thing, I knew my mom would be horribly disappointed if I dropped out. (My father had passed away in the summer between my freshman and sophomore years.) Besides that, I really had no plan for what would come next if I left school. My life, which had been pretty well mapped out to this point, was suddenly a blank page. The unknown future was like a bottomless pit beckoning me to jump in. The fear was all-consuming. But I knew I couldn't continue being miserable, doing work I hated for a man I did not respect and who treated me terribly.

I arranged a meeting with the dean of Engineering to explain what was going on. I was horribly nervous going in to see him, but the meeting went well. He was very understanding and I felt better after talking with him about leaving the program. Telling my mother was more difficult, but even she was completely supportive, which solidified my relief. Once I'd committed to the decision, it was like a huge weight had been lifted from my life and I felt empowered. That moment became an important life lesson for me. It made it easier for me the next time I was faced with a momentous decision. Which, in turn, made it easier for the time after that. Fear of the unknown keeps you from moving forward in life, I'd found. It's a useless and debilitating burden that should be jettisoned. I felt very lucky to have learned this early in life.

I stayed on for the rest of the school year as a part-time student, taking a couple of computer classes that interested me, and when spring came, I started looking for a job.

THE REAL WORLD

I ended up at Bell Laboratories in Naperville, Illinois, a suburb of Chicago. I chose this job because I'd been promised work that involved both hardware and software. In fact, the job involved neither—maybe just a little knowledge of each. I worked in the TSPS department, an acronym for Traffic Service Position System. You'd never guess from this name that it meant they developed software for the consoles that telephone operators used. You may be asking, "What's a telephone operator?" Well, operators were people who you'd reach by dialing "0" on your phone. They handled special types of calls like collect or person-to-person calls, or international long distance. In the 1970s, they sat at consoles with lots of square, multi-colored buttons and a numeric display.

Every few months there'd be revisions to this system with new features and upgrades, and Bell Labs would

TSPS Operator Console.

pick a phone company office somewhere in the country to use as a test site for the first installation of the latest revision. Other engineers did the actual hardware and software design. I was part of the testing team. The other testers and I would spend months writing up tests (procedures designed to test new features and make sure old features didn't break), then we'd go on-site for a few months and run those tests before the site went live, reporting bugs back to the developers who would then send us fixes to re-test.

Bell Labs had a requirement that their engineers have master's degrees. To ensure this, they had a program called OYOC (One Year On Campus), under which they sent me back to college. So, after only a few months on the job, I spent a year at Ohio State University on Bell Labs' dime, getting my MS in Electrical Engineering. I learned more practical information about computer design in that year than I ever would have if I'd stayed at RPI.

I returned from OSU to work that had both challenges and rewards. For example, I had a friend going to medical school in Israel, and I could place calls to him from a console whenever I wanted. International phone calls were pretty rare and very expensive back then. There was also something exciting about getting to live in a new city for a few months. I spent six months in Buffalo on my first project, and the following year I lived in Denver for five months. We were a very small team there and pretty much unsupervised, working odd shifts—sometimes overnight. As a single guy, I enjoyed this freedom and looseness. I've never really been a fan of sitting at a desk from 9 to 5.

When it came time to return from Denver, I didn't really want to leave. I'd made friends there, and it felt more like home than suburban Illinois. Still I had no choice. Once back, though, I requested to be transferred out of testing, and for a time I was loaned to an R&D department where I actually did some hardware design—building a pattern-matching system using micro-controllers for an early speech recognition prototype. This was the kind of work I wanted to be doing, and I got along well with the rest of the team. When I was told after a few months that I was being sent back into testing, I felt like the rug had been pulled out from under me. So I quit.

This was the second major decision of my adult life. And it came a little easier than the first, but there was still the question of "What's next?" I had nothing lined up as far as job prospects. I had saved some money so I could survive a few months, but after that . . . ?

I mentioned before that Naperville is a suburb of Chicago. Yet as a city boy, I much preferred heading into the Windy City on weekends rather than staying in the 'burbs. Sometimes, though, it was hard to find people to join me. Suburban folks seemed to think Chicago was a place you went to get murdered. But I managed to find a few brave souls to join me for treks into the city. We'd almost always end up in the Lincoln Park area to see *The Rocky Horror Picture Show* at the Biograph or a play at the Apollo Theater, or to listen to bands at any number of clubs on Lincoln Avenue.

With my new unemployment, there really wasn't anything keeping me in Naperville. So, late in the summer of 1981, I moved into the big city to the very neighborhood I'd come to feel so comfortable in—Lincoln Park. But what to do once I got there?

I'd seen some shows at the famous Second City improv/comedy theater and thought, "Hey, I can do that." So I asked at the box office where one would go to study improvisation, and they sent me to the only improv school that existed at the time, the Players Workshop of Second City.

I enrolled in a one-year improvisation class, which became the focal point of my life. I even thought it might be the start of a new career. You see, when I left Bell Labs, I wasn't just leaving that job. I felt that I was leaving computer engineering for good. I'd always felt a bit of an oddball at Bell Labs. Although I'd made some friends, and genuinely liked most of the people I worked with, there was something about me that was just different from most engineers. It was a culture of button-down shirts and ties, and staying as far away from the city as possible. They liked the security of their 9-to-5 lives. I shared their love of technical things, but I didn't speak in acronyms like most other engineers seemed fond of doing. Somehow I'd gotten it in my head that I just didn't belong in that world, and I took my exit from Bell Labs as a sign. I was going to leave the world of engineering behind and become . . . an actor.

I have to laugh at this recollection, because it's really the height of ballsiness to think that I could waltz into Chicago and start making money as an actor when my only experience had been three college plays and maybe a couple of community theater productions. And I wasn't even thinking of myself becoming a "real" actor (which, to my mind at the time, meant a dramatic actor), but rather a comedic actor. I thought I'd end up in a group like Monty Python or the Firesign Theatre.

So I went to my improv class and started learning from the best improv teachers in town. Okay, yes, they were also the *only* improv teachers in town, but they really were good. Martin de Maat, Judy Morgan, Linnea Forsberg, and the great Jo Forsberg, who had founded the school and was one of the pioneers of improv as an art form.

As money started to dwindle, I also looked for part-time survival work any place I could find it—with the exception of anything to do with engineering.

I worked for Encyclopedia Britannica, phoning people who'd mailed in cards embedded in various magazines, expressing an interest in purchasing a set of encyclopedias. I took this job specifically because it didn't involve sales. (I found the idea of trying to talk people into buying encyclopedias extremely distasteful.) But my bosses were impressed with my phone voice and manner, and within two days they promoted me . . . to sales. I didn't last the week. I also used my apparently fabulous voice to get some part-time work doing phone surveys for a radio station. But that got too depressing because most people assumed I was trying to sell them something, and those who didn't seemed to have just experienced some kind of tragedy. So I felt obligated to comfort them rather than just get off the phone and move to the next call. It was rough.

Winter didn't help things, as heavy snow and wind-chill temperatures well below zero degrees made job hunting difficult if not impossible. I would find myself leafing through the want ads in the Sunday paper each week, passing over the ones looking for engineers or software developers, but then slowly sort of glancing back at them. No harm in looking, right?

Still, I felt guilty. I'd made a commitment to leave engineering for good, and damn it, I was going to honor it.

CHAPTER TWO

ENTERING
WONDERLAND

On Sunday, December 27, 1981, having just spent Christmas alone and with my funds rapidly dwindling, I scanned the want ads in the *Chicago Tribune* and saw something that made me do a double take. There was an ad from a company seeking "Hardware/Software Engineers" with "strong interest and experience in video games and real-time interactive graphics."

I couldn't believe it at first—this seemed the least plausible way that a company would look for candidates for such a desirable job. But there it was, in black and white. The ad requested submissions be sent to "VIDEO MANIA c/o D. Gottlieb & Co.," makers of pinball machines

Chicago Tribune Dec. 27, 1981

Engineer

HARDWARE/SOFTWARE
ENGINEERS

Electronic amusement game manufacturer in west suburban location requires Microprocessor Hardware/ Software Engineers to expand our Video Entertainment engineering staff. Specialists with strong interest and experience in video games and real-time interactive graphics are needed.

If you are up to the challenge of designing video games, please send letter and/or resume detailing your skills and experience to:

VIDEO MANIA c/o

D. Gottlieb & Co.

A Columbia Pictures Industries Company

759 Industrial Drive
Bensenville, IL 60106

An Equal Opportunity
Employer M/F

This is the actual ad that appeared in the *Chicago Tribune* on Sunday, December 27, 1981. If I hadn't noticed and responded to it, my life would have turned out very differently.

since 1927. While I didn't have any experience to speak of, I certainly had a strong interest!

There were three jobs I'd always aspired to: making video games (since the day I saw the *Enterprise* shooting photon torpedoes on that oscilloscope at Brooklyn College), working for Walt Disney Imagineering (the R&D group for Disney), and working for NASA. (A fourth dream job, working on special effects for movies, came later.) The inclusion of NASA, the only non-entertainment-based job of the bunch, came from my fascination with space exploration, which fed into my desire to work on the Mars rover project in college. I never did get to work *for* NASA, but I did get to work *with* them to an extent on a game-related project in the mid-2000s. And I also got to work for Disney Imagineering for a brief and ultimately disappointing time.

But those experiences were way in the future. In 1981, the opportunity presenting itself was a job making video games. I balked at first. After all, I'd told myself I was through with engineering, having made the commitment to complete my improv training and start performing. And yet . . . what harm could it do to send in a resume? I didn't expect that they'd actually call me in for an interview, and if they did, I could always turn it down. I'd made two major decisions in my life so far—dropping out of the master's program at RPI and quitting my job at Bell Labs—and I felt that no choice I made was irreversible. If something didn't work out, I could just choose something else.

So I sent in my resume with a very informal cover letter that may have projected—how should I put this?—some indifference on my part. I figured if they didn't like my laid-back and "unprofessional" nature, then I probably wouldn't like working there anyway.

To my surprise, I got a response in the mail that same

week, just before New Year's Day! The letter asked me to come in for an interview as soon as possible. I considered whether or not I should accept, but once again I asked myself: What harm could it do? They wouldn't necessarily offer me a job after the interview, and if they did, I could always turn it down. I made an appointment for the following week.

Their offices in Bensenville were in an industrial park on the far side of O'Hare Airport. Not much to look at, really—gray and nondescript, much like the entire neighborhood. I dressed very informally for the interview, again motivated by my disdain for the kind of "shirt and tie" environment I did not want to return to. As I walked from the parking lot to the front entrance, I passed by a very large, rotund man with a Vandyke and a gravelly voice. He asked if I was there for an interview. When I said yes, his response was, "Watch out for that Waxman guy. He's a real hard-ass." Okay, good to know, I guess. I wasn't sure whether to worry or be grateful.

The first person I met with was a middle-management type named Bill Jacobs, my guide throughout the process. He was friendly and personable, and he wore a suit. (I took this as a bad sign.) He took me around the place, which consisted of a large, empty manufacturing plant and a small set of adjacent offices. The offices were sparsely furnished, and there was one pretty big room that housed a few people and a lot of equipment. The room was open—no cubicles or makeshift walls, just tables. I met one engineer who wore a shirt and tie and spoke to me in acronyms. I flashed back to Bell Labs and my dislike of that habit, and the thought that I would hate working here grew stronger.

But then I met a few more people who seemed less like engineers, and more like . . . well, normal people. They were mostly programmers and hardware guys; one or two were artists. I felt a little more relaxed. Eventually, I was taken to a conference room where I was to meet with the Vice President of Engineering, Ron Waxman. I prepared myself to meet the "hard-ass."

When he arrived, I was somewhat surprised to see that he was, in fact, the very same rotund man who had warned me about Waxman earlier. He sat at one end of the long conference table, and I sat at the other. Being very large, he didn't move much. When he spoke, his voice was just as gravelly as before, and somewhat monotone. He stared at me for an uncomfortably long time before speaking.

"What makes you think you can program video games?" he asked. I detected a tinge of smugness in his voice.

Okay, so much for niceties. Still, I wasn't put off by the question. My ambivalence about working there gave me a kind of protection from getting too emotionally invested in this conversation.

"I don't know," I said. "I've never done it. I've always wanted to, though."

"Do you have a computer a home?" he asked.

"No."

"Why not?" Every question had a subtext of contempt.

"Well, I use them at work. I never felt a need to have one at home." Keep in mind, this was 1982—there really were not a lot of people who had computers in their homes. Just hard-core hobbyists. Even the IBM PC, which had been introduced earlier that year, was considered an office product.

He asked questions about my schooling and work at Bell Labs, what video games I played and liked, and with every question came a pre-supposition of an unsatisfactory answer. My answers were as calm and truthful as I could make them. If he didn't like them, it was no skin off my nose. I really had nothing to lose.

After that interview, Bill Jacobs cheerfully thanked me for coming in, and I left knowing with absolute certainty that I had not impressed that hard-ass Waxman. But they must have popped the offer letter in the mail almost instantly, as I received it a couple of days later. I panicked. It seems ridiculous to me now that this was such a difficult decision, but I was really enjoying the improv program at Players Workshop and still had a strong aversion to a structured environment like Bell Labs. As I wrestled with the commitment I was considering making, the thought kept coming back to me: I could always quit. That became my anchor. Any time it seemed that I'd made the wrong choice, I could just quit. And if it turned out that I liked working there, it would be a dream come true.

I squashed the panic and accepted.

BENSENVILLE

I started work at D. Gottlieb & Co. on January 11, 1982. (My ID badge had a typo on it—it said 1981.) I was promptly set up at a workbench in the "lab," the big, open

My first Gottlieb business card. I tried to get a non-traditional job title printed, like "Techno-Geek" or "Software Dude," but no luck.

shared room I'd been taken to during my interview. Among the projects going on when I started was a pinball machine called *Caveman*, which was the first pin to incorporate a video game played on a 13-inch monitor within the playfield. Another was *Quizimodo*, an Apple II-based quiz game intended for bars. And there were a couple of arcade video games under development that ran on Gottlieb's recently designed hardware.

Gottlieb came into the arcade video game market relatively late. Their first two games, *New York! New York!* and *No Man's Land*, were licensed from Japan and did not sell very well. At some point, the decision was made to build an in-house team in Bensenville, which was ironically about eight miles away from Gottlieb's main offices and pinball assembly line in Northlake, Illinois. The men tasked to lead the new group were Howie Rubin, VP of Business Development, and Ron Waxman, VP of Engineering. Sometime during 1980, they started with a few current employees and began hiring new ones. But finding anyone with experience (let alone success) in making a video game was difficult.

Fortunately, in 1981, they brought in a multi-talented designer-programmer-artist with a track record of making successful games: Tim Skelly. Tim's resume included *Rip Off, Star Castle,* and *Armor Attack,* all made by Cinematronics. Somehow, Howie and Ron had convinced Tim to come over to Gottlieb to show the fledgling video department how it's done. Hardware designer Jun Yum developed a sprite-based hardware based on Intel's 8088 CPU (Central Processing Unit), and Tim began developing a concept that became the game *Reactor*. The CPU was the heart of any computer system. The 8088 was also the CPU used in the original IBM PC.

Reactor was pretty much done when I came on board in January of 1982. It was just entering the process of field-testing, which would result in some tweaks and changes by Tim. And here I was, green as I could be, and in need of some training. Although Tim had his hands full, he was still very much a mentor to the rest of us. For one thing, he projected a real rock-star aura, and most of the guys on the staff were, well, kind of nerds. Myself included. Tim had the confidence of someone who had tasted success and was operating at the top of their form, but he was also approachable. And generous. He gave a lot of the utility code he had written for *Reactor* to others for use in their games.

I was handed over to Tom Malinowski, who was in the middle of programming a game of his own design. He needed help with some supplemental tasks so he could focus on the more important aspects of the game. His concept was based on the movie *Superman II*, wherein Superman fights three villains from his home planet, Krypton. Superman, however, was a property of DC Comics, which was owned by Warner Brothers; Gottlieb (at the time) was owned by Columbia Pictures. The idea of Columbia licensing a property from a competitor was distasteful. Plus, Howie Rubin had previously worked for Atari and had had some bad experiences there in the development of the 1979 Superman pinball machine. So with a Superman game being particularly unlikely, Howie contacted Columbia's licensing department to see if it could get the rights to any superhero. The answer was no, and as Howie puts it, "We tested some waters, but were not very aggressive."

So without an actual superhero to license, Tom had no choice but to create his own. Jeff Lee, who provided the graphics for the game, has a copy of a design doc handwritten by Tom and dated January of 1981, called "Super-Hero." Whether Tom was hopeful to get the Superman license at that time or knew that it was never going to happen is unclear. But sometime in 1981, he got the green light to proceed with his concept. Jeff designed a suitably generic superhero character, and Tom was off and running.

So what was the game? Well, our unnamed hero battles a bunch of super-villains but can't kill them; his main goal is to protect pedestrians on the street. The player uses a trackball to fly around. Most of the screen is just empty sky to fly through, but on the right and left sides of the screen are buildings. Other locations appear in later levels, notably a bridge. On the bottom of the screen is a street/sidewalk where pedestrians and vehicles pass from one side to the other. The villains can fly into the buildings, creating rubble that blasts out and falls somewhere on the street, potentially crushing pedestrians. They can also grab and carry pedestrians away or pick up vehicles to drop on them. Superman—er, I mean our hero—can grab pedestrians and cars from a villain by crashing into him, then return them safely to the ground. He can also pulverize falling rubble before it hits the ground. There were more features, but I'm not sure if they were part of the initial design or came later. This game would eventually go through at least four iterations and have four different titles in its struggle to reach the production line.

Tom assigned me to deal with the rubble that fell and piled up on the street when the game's villains crash into buildings. Video games are like movies in that they are essentially a sequence of still images displayed fast enough for the eye to perceive them as motion. While movies traditionally played at 24 frames per second, our video games refreshed 60 times each second. In the case of our two-dimensional, sprite-based system, each sprite was a 16-by-16 grid of pixels. The sprites would be positioned at specific coordinates on the screen for each frame. To create motion, the programmer just needed to adjust those coordinates between frames. And Jun's hardware made it pretty easy to do that. Before you knew it, I had programmed falling rubble.

The problem was . . . what to do with these piles of rubble? As they accumulated, they eventually covered the street, leaving no room for new rubble and using up foreground objects (sprites that our hardware could display in limited quantity). Looking back, I can't remember why we didn't just have rubble disappear after a few seconds. It's possible we may have tried that and Tom didn't like the way it looked. Whatever the reason, we didn't do it, so I programmed a bulldozer to emerge from one side of the screen and push the rubble sprites out of view. When enough rubble accumulated, the bulldozer reappeared, moving in the opposite direction to repeat the task.

The video graphics were done by Jeff Lee, who was the go-to artist in Gottlieb's video division. As affable as a fellow can be and extraordinarily talented, with a taste for the surreal and whimsical that I always found appealing, Jeff worked miracles with the blocky pixels available to him. There were a couple of proprietary software tools written to aid in creating video game art—FOGUS for creating those 16-by-16-pixel foreground sprites which could appear anywhere on screen, and BOGUS for background blocks, which were 8-by-8 pixels and fit into a grid that made up the background. Our screen was 256 by 240 pixels, so the background grid contained 32 columns and 30 rows.

Jeff did a fantastic job with all of the graphics for Tom's game, but of particular note was his crafting of the pedestrians who walked back and forth on the street. Each one of them was unique, not just in their look, but in the way they walked and carried themselves. That he could accomplish this with so few pixels and colors (16 total) is truly amazing. (And as a tidbit of trivia, the guy with the Afro and beard is me.)

In addition to the rubble and bulldozer, I also worked on the diagnostics for the game. This was a mode that could only be entered when the coin door was open. A switch inside the cabinet allowed an operator to put the game into a Diagnostic Mode, where they would get a menu consisting of tests (i.e. Memory, Sound, Switch, and Sprite tests) and settings (Difficulty, Extra Life Level, Number of Lives Per Coin, etc.). This was also a good learning experience for me since it involved all aspects of the hardware.

At some point, the game became ready for testing outside of Gottlieb, but it needed a name. And that name was: *Protector*. Presumably, "Super-hero" was a little too meta for that era. In fact, the term "meta" wasn't even known then, except as a prefix.

As I mentioned earlier, Gottlieb's video game division was working out of a separate plant from pinball—one with a large manufacturing area currently sitting empty. *Reactor* was being field-tested in local arcades and Tim Skelly was still making adjustments to it, but it would be some months before it started production. And though at that time Gottlieb didn't enforce deadlines or milestones on any project—adopting a freedom it would, in some cases, regret later—management was keenly aware that once the production line started rolling, it needed to keep rolling. Shutting down the production line meant laying off workers and losing momentum, which translated into lost revenue. The pinball industry was used to ups and downs, but it always did what it could to keep the line rolling—usually by lowering the production output (the number of games built per day) rather than shutting down completely. So management was very hopeful that after *Reactor*, *Protector* would be the second in-house game released. Field-testing in local arcades was essential for any new game, for a couple of reasons. First, we (those of us working on the game) would often go to the arcade and watch people play. This is not as creepy as it sounds—watching other people play a new game was common. But while others would watch just to see what the new game was about or how good the current player was, we would watch to see how the player responded to the game. Did they understand the controls easily? Did they get frustrated? Did it seem too hard? Too easy? Were they having fun? Any number of us might go to watch a game on test, but it was up to the designer/programmer to make any changes. Management and others might offer advice or suggestions, but the programmer was the one to fix it.

The second valuable piece of information we got from field-testing was monetary. How many quarters were going into the coin box? New games almost always tended to get a lot of play initially as players checked them out. After a week or so, if the numbers dropped, that was a clear indication that players weren't coming back. Another way to get feedback on a game was through focus groups. There'd be a small group of people in a room with a one-way mirror who would play the game for a while, then sit down and answer questions posed to them by a moderator.

Unfortunately, the test results were not good for *Protector*. There are a number of factors that may have contributed. One was that you controlled *Protector* with a trackball instead of a joystick. Precision was likely an issue, as was the lack of any force feedback when you slammed into a villain. Another problem was in the design. You couldn't actually harm the villains—the best you could do was knock them away or keep them from succeeding at whatever mayhem they were attempting. Some players found that unsatisfying.

It didn't help that the game suffered from some technical issues, due mostly to Tom's inexperience as a programmer. Kan Yabumoto, a fellow Gottlieb programmer best known as the creator of *Mad Planets*, believed that poor memory management caused slowdowns. Since video games operated on a 60-hertz loop, meaning that the screen refreshed every 1/60 of a second, whatever processing you had to do in order to fill the frame needed to be done within that time. If your processing took longer, you'd miss the refresh and the game would appear to stutter.

But management so believed in the potential of this game that they refused to give up on it. Jeff Lee has a thirteen-page memo with notes from a meeting on March 29, 1982—attended by a number of us, myself included—which contain, as Jeff puts it, "An excruciatingly detailed discussion of gameplay possibilities." Tom did his best to accommodate suggestions, and made changes dutifully.

The first change was to the name, from *Protector* to *Videoman*. Why? Not sure. Perhaps so that when it went out on test again, players would think it was a completely new game. Even if they recognized it, the new title might imply that the game itself had changed enough to encourage players to give it another go. When *Videoman* didn't catch on, the next version became *Guardian*. Still no improvement. Next, in an attempt to give the main character a non-generic identity, they went with the more specific yet arbitrary and puzzling *Argus*.

Dave Thiel, who did the sounds for this game, recalls a focus group that resulted in the trackball being changed to a joystick. According to him, "Players didn't understand what was unsatisfying about the interaction, so they reached out to the familiar and insisted that a joystick would fix it." A shooting attack was added. I think it was supposed to be like Superman's heat vision, but we had a sprite-based system, so it looked more like projectiles. At some point, the game was modified to allow the player to kill the villains. In one version, presumably the last, the rubble was removed. Instead, strange "energy spikes" came down from above and would zap pedestrians if they touched one, adding yet another danger they needed protection from.

After months of changes to gameplay, graphics, and titles, the game was becoming something of an internal joke. I started calling it *Pro-Vid-Guard-Argus*. I'm not sure exactly when the plug got pulled, but pulled it eventually got. Management was very disappointed, as I'm sure Tom was. I'm told that some version of *Pro-Vid-Guard-Argus* is available to play using MAME, which is awesome. Gotta love MAME. And just recently, Doc Mack, owner of the Galloping Ghost arcade in Brookfield, Illinois, helped Tom and Jeff restore a version of the game (called just *Argus*) in a working arcade cabinet with an original marquee and cabinet art.

There's another version of *Pro-Vid-Guard-Argus* I haven't mentioned yet. With all the conversations, hand-wringing, and hair-pulling that went into figuring out how to make this concept fly (no pun intended), someone thought maybe the answer was to go a comical route. And to that end, Jeff Lee created the superhero WaxMan, who bore an astonishing resemblance to Gottlieb's VP of Engineering, Ron Waxman. The rotund hero was swapped into the game and a marquee was created, but as far as I know, this version of the game was always intended as a joke and never tested (although I'm pretty sure Howie Rubin lobbied for it). In fact, Jeff Lee says he has drawings in his archives of "a couple of other fat guys in costume which are *not* Waxman."

My involvement with *Pro-Vid-Guard-Argus* had ended with the rubble and diagnostics, and in April of 1982, I was without a project. Management (meaning Howie and Ron) tasked me with a simple goal: make us a video game.

The staff was pretty small then. I mentioned that Jeff Lee was the go-to artist at the company; I'm pretty sure he was the only one who did nothing but video graphics. There were a couple of programmers who did their own artwork—Tim Skelly for one, and Chris Brewer, who would become co-creator of *M.A.C.H. 3*, Gottlieb's hugely successful LaserDisc game. But for all of the other programmers who were not artistically inclined, Jeff was the man.

For hardware, other than Jun Yum, there was Jim Weisz (who worked on *Caveman*, the pinball/video hybrid). Dave Thiel was our only sound guy. On the programming side, besides myself and the aforementioned Tom Malinowski, Kan Yabumoto, Chris Brewer, and Tim Skelly, we had Sam Russo (who programmed *Quizimodo*) and a fellow named Fred Darmstadt (the other co-creator of *M.A.C.H. 3*). That was basically it, and we all had the same broad and non-specific mandate: make a video game.

The amazing thing about Howie and Ron's management style was that they knew they *didn't* know what made a video game good or successful. They knew we were in the wild, wild west of video game development, and that you couldn't just look back and copy what had already been done. You had to come up with something new, and they trusted that, as a group, we could (with Tim's guidance) do that. When I say "we," I'm speaking specifically about the programmers in the group. In Gottlieb's model, the programmers were the game designers. This may have been somewhat frustrating for Jeff Lee, who would never be able to get a programmer to back any game ideas he may have had, but as a policy it didn't last long. Later, as the department grew, some "designers" were hired, but for now the programmers led their projects.

Another thing Howie and Ron were good at was protecting us from upper management. Any internal politics or pressures coming from above lay squarely on their shoulders, and we in the trenches never knew about it. Life was always good in our little Bensenville bubble. In the days before *Reactor* rolled off the production line, when the massive manufacturing area was largely empty, Howie would come into the lab and announce loudly, "Okay everybody—stop what you're doing!" When he'd gotten our attention, he'd add, "We're going down to the plant to play some football." And off we'd go.

The looseness of the environment was especially pleasing to me and made it easier to keep us on task. It really didn't take long for me to realize that my fears of going back to an "engineering" environment were unfounded. We had no pressures, no deadlines. We were expected to be self-motivated, and by and large I think we all were. We operated in some ways like a think tank: explore ideas, and maybe they'll work out, maybe not. It was a luxury, albeit one that couldn't (and didn't) last forever.

I mentioned that our game hardware was based on an 8088 processor. To access its program and image memory for development, we used a system made by Intel that was housed in a large, royal-blue desktop box. We referred to it as "The Blue Box." (I know, not very imaginative, but accurate.) It had a long cable that plugged into our hardware where the CPU chip would normally be. This technique was called In-Circuit Emulation (ICE).

Its storage system, which we used to save programs and image data, was a 9-inch-square floppy disk drive. And these were the truly floppy kind. By way of comparison, the original IBM PC used 5 ¼-inch (truly) floppy disks, and later the standard became 3 ¾-inch floppies in a hard case, so not really floppy at all. I think we only had three or four of these Blue Boxes. Not enough for each programmer to have his own, so we had to share them.

All of the programming we did was in assembly language, which is as close to a computer's natural language (or "machine language") as possible. There were no complicated mathematical functions available. There were no floating-point co-processors. Things like finding a square root or computing a sine or cosine were dependent on algorithms we would have to code ourselves and which would run ridiculously slowly. We tried to avoid these functions if possible, and used look-up tables if absolutely necessary to make them faster. Since CPU time was a precious commodity, we would "count cycles" (cycles are a measure of CPU time) for any given routine and employ every bit of creativity to reduce them. Programmers would pride themselves on coming up with the fastest square root or random number routine, and show it off to other programmers.

Memory was scarce. Our system had 64 kilobytes for the program, 64 kilobytes for foreground sprite artwork, and 32 kilobytes for background blocks. Granted, this was much more than a typical home system like the Atari 2600 had, but arcade games were like Maseratis compared to the Toyota Corolla-like home games.

With *Pro-Vid-Guard-Argus* behind me, and now having a basic understanding of our video game hardware and how to program it, it was my job to try and build a Maserati.

CHAPTER THREE

THE CUBES GAME

I've always been a fan of M. C. Escher. In college, I had a couple of his posters on my dorm room wall. There was something about the fantastic nature of his drawings that captured my imagination. Beyond the beauty in their symmetry and the draftsman-like precision, some are puzzles, impossible to exist in the real world. And while I knew I wasn't alone in my appreciation of his work (he was very popular back then), I didn't know that Jeff Lee, the video graphic artist who had worked magic on *Pro-Vid-Guard-Argus*, was also a fan.

One day in the spring of 1982, with *Pro-Vid-Guard-Argus* behind me and my only task being to "make a video game," I noticed something up on the screen of fellow programmer Kan Yabumoto's workstation. At the time, Kan was experimenting with a feature of our hardware that allowed the background to appear in front of the foreground. He seemed to be playing with the notion of removing parts of the background to reveal something behind it. This turned out to be kind of a nifty feature that I would soon take advantage of as well. But what really caught my eye was the image Kan was using as his "background." It was a full screen of repeating Escher-like cubes created for him by Jeff Lee.

Our hardware supported a background made up of 8-by-8 pixel "blocks," which were placed in a grid 32 blocks across and 30 blocks down for a horizontally mounted monitor or, if you oriented the monitor vertically, 30 across and 32 down. Using a repeating pattern of 4-by-4 background blocks, Jeff was able to fill the screen with cubes from edge to edge. Since memory was a precious commodity in those days, anything you could do to reuse a piece of art was helpful, so it was pretty clever of Jeff to get a full screen with only 16 blocks.

This cube pattern was remarkable for a number of reasons. First of all, I recognized the Escher-ness of the design and appreciated it. Second, Jeff's use of primary colors for the cube faces made it look bright and cartoony. Third and most importantly, the pseudo-3D look of the cubes gave an illusion of depth you didn't normally see on a video game screen in those days. The very first video game to use that type of illusion—known as isometric projection and sometimes called "2 ½D"—was *Zaxxon*, which had only recently made its debut in January 1982.

There was something else I noticed about the cube pattern that was serendipitous, although at the time it was just a random thought. Here I was, a fairly green programmer with no real game experience other than the few tasks I'd done on *Pro-Vid-Guard-Argus*. I wanted to learn something more—something that could be a handy skill on whatever game I was about to make. One obvious choice was gravity. In *Pro-Vid-Guard-Argus*, the rubble that got knocked out of the buildings fell at a constant rate. That is, its position changed vertically by the same number of pixels (its "velocity") each frame. I wanted to be able to create something closer to real-world physics, or at least as much as our limited computing power would allow.

Trigonometric functions were prohibitively slow to calculate. The best you could hope for was a stored table with all possible values pre-computed. But that used up memory—also a precious commodity. Luckily, there was a crude way to implement gravity that wouldn't waste either memory or computing cycles. Just as each object on the screen moved by adding its velocity to its position each frame, gravity (or any acceleration) worked by adding the acceleration to the velocity each frame. I just needed to implement it, and see it in action.

As I looked at the cubes, it occurred to me that if you dropped a ball on the top of a cube, it could be programmed to bounce down to the cube on the next lower level, and again and again, all the way down to the bottom. Looking at the cube pattern, it also became clear that each bounce presented the ball with exactly two choices of where to go next: right or left. Having two choices is something programmers tend to like. The world of computers essentially boils down to bits (short for "binary digits"), namely 0 and 1. The basis of all computer memory is the byte, which is simply 8 bits. A single choice of going right or left could be represented by 1 bit, and a single byte (8 choices) could predetermine the entire path of a ball from top to bottom.

Now it was getting interesting. Balls could conceivably fall onto any cube at any time, but that seemed too chaotic for me. The last thing I wanted to do was complicate anything. However, if every ball fell on the same first cube, there were only two cubes that could be the next choice. From those two cubes, a ball could only fall on three cubes below. It suddenly became very clear—what I needed was a pyramid of cubes.

I set about figuring how many cubes I could fit on the screen. Turned out I could fit more rows of cubes on a vertically mounted monitor (seven, in fact). Next, the current set of background blocks was designed to repeat, so I needed blocks to represent the edges of the pyramid. I don't call myself an artist, but these blocks were very simple, so it was easy enough to plop down black pixels where necessary and create edge blocks using our background tool, BOGUS. Next I needed a ball, and Jeff supplied me with a lovely orange one.

You may ask ... why have the pyramid just floating in space? Why not have it be part of some other structure or location? Well, again, simplicity is the answer. This was just a programming exercise and I wanted to keep things as simple as possible. It didn't take long before I had a ball falling with gravity. The tricky part was detecting a collision with the cube top surface and redirecting the ball for another bounce. But I figured it out. And it looked pretty cool. I was simulating real-world physics on a video monitor!

Yes, I'm a programming geek. These kinds of things get my endorphins going.

What I needed next was a way for each ball to have a unique, seemingly random path. Since the path of each ball was determined by a byte representing a series of "bounce right" and "bounce left" instructions, what I really needed was a string of random bytes. In programming terms, that's called a random number generator. Tim Skelly was kind enough to give me the one he'd used in *Reactor*. Whenever a ball was about to fall, I asked his subroutine for a random byte. At every bounce, I'd look at the next bit to determine whether the ball should bounce to the right or left.

When I was done, I had a pyramid of cubes floating in space with balls dropping from the top of the screen, landing on the top cube, then bouncing randomly down the pyramid and disappearing off the bottom of the screen to an unknown place. It was extraordinarily satisfying to have accomplished this, but something didn't look quite right. Balls landing on a cube didn't respond visually to that contact. I mean, when a rubber ball hits a hard surface, you'd expect the ball's shape to deform slightly as a result of the force of the contact with that surface. I was using a single image of a perfectly round ball, so there was no deformation. But they bounced, so clearly they weren't hard like a bowling ball, although visually they might as well have been. It just seemed wrong.

I asked Jeff to create a ball with a slightly flattened bottom and figured out how to replace the perfectly round one with the flattened one when the ball made contact with a cube top. Now the illusion seemed pretty perfect! It was a subtle thing, but it made a huge difference (to me, at least). Whether anyone else at Gottlieb noticed this little detail is uncertain, but they certainly noticed the simulation as a whole and commented on how cool it looked.

But still, it wasn't a game. For one thing, it needed a player character. Once again, I went to Jeff and asked if he'd made any characters that weren't being used for something else. Turned out, he had a few. He put them up on a screen for me to look at, and I was immediately struck by the one that looked kind of innocent (perhaps even pathetic?), with a long nose and no arms. Jeff designed him that way thinking he'd shoot projectiles out of his nose. As much as I liked the goofiness of that idea, I really didn't see any need for shooting anything at this point. I just wanted a character that could jump from cube to cube. Jeff then created all the variations of the orange character that I'd need (facing in each possible direction). And just as I'd asked of the orange ball, I requested accompanying images of the character with his knees retracted a bit, so it looked like they absorbed the impact of landing on a cube. Later on, when *Q*bert* was ported to consumer game platforms, I was dismayed to see that little touch omitted from some of the ports.

Once I had the artwork I needed, I set about coding

the joystick to get the player character moving from cube to cube. But a small problem arose. Most joysticks are 4-way—up, down, left, and right. Some joysticks are 8-way, able to sense diagonal directions by activating two of the 4 switches at once. But from the design of my playfield, it was clear that what I needed was a 4-way joystick that *only* reported diagonal motion. After all, my player character couldn't jump straight up or straight down or perfectly left or right.

As I mentioned earlier, I was developing my software on the Intel Blue Box connected to our video game hardware through a cable. But our hardware wasn't mounted inside of a game cabinet like it would be when you saw it in an arcade. It was just a large circuit board sitting loose on a table, connected by a mass of wires to a monitor that was also sitting on the table. Having no cabinet meant I had no control panel, which hadn't been a problem up till now because I hadn't needed one. But now I did.

What would typically happen at this point is a programmer would request whatever controller they needed from our engineering technician, and they would rig up a temporary housing for it. I ended up getting a 4-way joystick mounted in an upside-down, square plastic bucket. This joystick, whether by habit or because it was the established norm, was mounted with each direction aligned to an edge of the container. Since my needs were different, I just rotated the bucket 45 degrees and I was off and running.

THE FIRST MANTRA

Programming the player's motion was a lot of fun. Getting the "physics" to feel right took some time, and I had to make a decision about what to do if a player jumped off the pyramid. Should I just keep him stuck at the edge, or allow him to fall into nothingness? I chose the latter because of that cool feature that Kan had used to switch foreground and background. When a player jumped off the pyramid and was at the apex of his jump, I removed all other foreground objects, made the switch and let gravity take over. The poor orange guy looked as if he was falling behind the pyramid! It was another subtle but perfect illusion. As I play-tested this, I actually liked the tension that it added to the experience. Let's face it, every video game (especially an arcade game) has to have some way for the player to die, or the game will never end. Staying on the pyramid seemed like a skill that players could and should be able to master.

Now I had balls bouncing down the pyramid and a controllable player moving all around it. I asked myself the question that became my first design mantra: "What's next?"

Having never designed a video game before, I wasn't so arrogant as to think I could be an expert at it immediately. And thankfully, Howie and Ron didn't ask (at least not yet) for written game design documents. They really gave the programmers free rein to explore and develop their ideas. As it turned out, this strategy worked for some games, but not for others.

Luckily, it was working for me.

So what was next? Well, the player and balls didn't interact. There was no collision detection between them. It would be nice if the balls were an obstacle that the player had to avoid. So I set about writing code to detect collisions between ball and player and "kill" the player on such an occasion. This proved to be challenging because, while the game looked like it was happening in a 3D world with depth, this was just an illusion. The screen was strictly two-dimensional. If I didn't get this right, the game would seem unfair, and I absolutely didn't want that. Being a video game player myself, I hated games that seemed unfair. So I worked on it until I felt I'd gotten it right. The balls became dangerous, but the player could learn to avoid them. And once again, I asked myself, "What's next?"

I'm not sure how much time had elapsed since I'd started this little programming exercise, which now appeared to be turning into a game. I would guess maybe two or three weeks. Howie Rubin loves to tell the story about how he went away on a business trip for a week and when he came back, here was this game, almost fully formed out of nowhere. I don't think it was *that* abrupt. I was just working under the radar. Whatever I was doing was not an official project. I was just tinkering. And although people around the office had seen what I was doing and thought it showed promise, no one (including me) knew where it was going or what it could become.

Ron Waxman, our beloved VP of Engineering, had a habit of coming by the big workroom that those of us without individual offices called home once the normal workday had ended. It wasn't uncommon for people to work late every now and then. Waxman always seemed to be in the office till 9:00 PM or so. I liked to stay late sometimes just because it was quieter and easier to think. One night, I was playing with what I'd programmed, jumping around the pyramid and avoiding balls, trying to decide what the next step would be. I knew what I had was fun and looked cool, but I also realized that in order for it to be a game, there needed to be a goal . . . something the player needed to accomplish, something more than what I currently had.

Waxman sat in a chair behind me. He usually had a cigar in hand, and you could hear him breathing. It was almost a wheeze—something akin to a Darth Vader

Creating Q*bert

breath. He was a large man and didn't move much unless he had to, so the breathing seemed to come from nowhere. It was unnerving at first, but you got used to it. As I was playing my not-yet-a-game, thinking about what to do next, I heard his gravelly voice behind me calmly say, "What if the cubes change color when he lands on them?"

I should talk a bit about getting ideas from other people, because that played a huge role in the development of Q*bert. I describe the process of creating Q*bert as "evolutionary" because each element was added after the previous element had been implemented. The environment at Gottlieb was open—not only physically, in that most of the development took place in a large open room—but also because everyone saw everyone else's work and felt free to comment or offer suggestions. For someone like Tim Skelly, who had a track record as a game designer, suggestions from all of us inexperienced wannabes must have been greeted with polite chagrin. But as I said earlier, I was not so arrogant as to think I had all the answers. Most of the time, I had ideas for what should be next. Other times, not so much. Later on, when I looked back at the experience, I likened my design approach to being a filter through which all ideas entered, yet only the ones I liked passed through. This isn't so different from the way many film directors work. They hire department heads such as art directors, cinematographers, editors, and sound designers and mixers who, based on their talent and experience, bring in ideas to best serve the director's vision. The director typically has the final say in deciding what ideas stay or go. Jeff was the primary alternative voice I had at the beginning, but I was willing to hear what anyone had to say.

As I was developing the game that would become Q*bert, I was offered many suggestions. I listened to all of them, and decided whether each one had merit. In doing so, I was limited not only by the technical constraints of memory and processor speed, but by my own inexperience. I was learning as I went along, and my second mantra became: "Keep it simple!"

Some ideas I rejected because they didn't appeal to me. Others I rejected because I couldn't see how to implement them. And then there were the ideas that clicked, and I embraced them. As soon as the words came out of Waxman's mouth, I knew he'd hit upon something. It made perfect sense to me, and in that moment, this "thing" I was working on, this exercise, became a game.

Mind you, it still didn't have a name. I simply referred to it as "the Cubes Game," knowing this would have to change later. But for now, I needed to keep moving forward. Sometime shortly after this, the game became an official project and was put on the schedule. I was its only

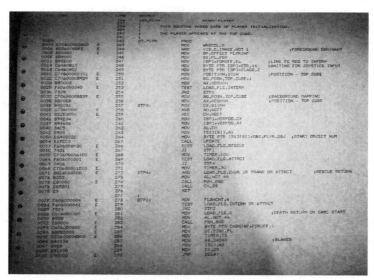

Some of the original Q*bert code printout. This section shows the ST_PLYR (Start Player) subroutine which initializes the player on top of the pyramid. Notice that nowhere in the code does the name Q*bert appear. The player character was referred to as "Plyr" and Coily was referred to as "Chsr" (Chaser).

Creating Q*bert

programmer and, as was the case with Gottlieb's video game division at the time, also the project leader and game designer.

SO IT'S A GAME. NOW WHAT?

The goal of changing the cube tops to a target color led to the game's structure and more of its play elements, such as the green ball that froze everything (giving you time to finish off a screen), and the impish nuisances, Slick and Sam, who would change cubes back to their original color. The idea of an enemy chasing the player was an obvious one. Jeff thought of using a coiled snake, and I coded it to arrive as a purple ball so the player had time to position himself strategically before it transformed into Coily. I loved pretty much everything about Jeff's artwork, and never objected to any of his character designs. Coily needed to be bigger than a typical sprite, so he's actually made up of two foreground objects, one on top of another.

Jeff, though technically not responsible for the game design and working on artwork for other games simultaneously, became my trusted collaborator and sounding board. We worked well together, and even though I nixed some of his ideas, I also graciously accepted others. The swearing cartoon balloon when the as-yet-unnamed player dies, as well as the discs used as an escape from Coily, were, I'm pretty sure, both Jeff Lee contributions. I say "pretty sure" because as the game began to progress quickly, we constantly built on each other's ideas as we discussed them.

At some point, the idea of shooting out of the player's nose was re-introduced. Jeff went so far as to write up a design document for a game that was jokingly called

Snots and Boogers, but I never seriously considered it. For one thing, programming the collision detection would have been a nightmare. For another, as the game had developed, I just didn't see the need for shooting. Avoiding obstacles, staying on the pyramid, and changing colors seemed like enough of a challenge. Also, one of the things I loved about *Pac-Man* was that you could play it with one hand. If you were in a bar, you could play it while you were holding a drink. Adding a "shoot" button meant you couldn't do that.

Jeff also had an idea that I originally dismissed as insane. He thought it'd be cool to have enemies whose gravity was aligned with the sides of the cubes, rather than the top. So instead of falling from the top of the screen, they'd "fall" from the lower left and right corners, bouncing "down" as if the cube was rotated in different directions. And while I could see this being a great visual, it seemed impossible from a programming point of view. I couldn't begin to fathom how to make the physics work without trigonometry or other advanced math functions that we just didn't have the power to compute. And even if I could get them bouncing in these alternate gravities, the collision detection presented such a nightmare scenario that my brain short-circuited trying to envision a solution.

But for some reason, the idea stuck in my head. Damn that Jeff Lee! My mind was working on solving this problem even when I didn't want it to be. At some point this became a nut I needed to crack. I think it was just the audacity of the idea that intrigued me. Of course, I did eventually figure out a way to make it work, and the purple characters now known as Ugg and Wrong-Way were introduced into the game, although it wasn't easy. The collision detection in particular took a lot of tweaking, and I was terrified that players would die from

Creating Q*bert

colliding with them without knowing how or why. So I tried to make those collisions very generous in favor of the player.

More elements were added to the game, and more of our in-house personnel stopped by to play it. And to my consternation, the first thing they'd do was rotate the bucket, holding the joystick so it wasn't diagonal. This would throw the axes off-kilter and make the game hard to control. I had to explain why it needed to be at a 45-degree angle and that usually solved the problem, but sometimes I'd get flak about it. I wasn't really concerned, though. I fully believed that when the joystick was mounted properly in a cabinet, this confusion would be eliminated. Ah, I was so naive back then.

SOUNDS

With the Cubes Game now official, more resources were assigned to it. I was given a sound programmer, David Thiel, who was responsible for the game's audio. Being new to video game development, I didn't really think much about game sounds, but I communicated to Dave as best I could where I thought I might need them, occasionally making awkward attempts to vocalize them. Dave was great at interpreting my sonic discharges and turning them into audio producible by our sound hardware. And of course he came up with a lot of the sounds on his own. While most of Dave's contributions to the game were sound-related, I also came to trust his opinions and sought his input as development progressed.

Since our big-nosed orange player character solicited empathy, it seemed appropriate that he should have a voice. There was a chip on our soundboard (the Votrax SC-01A) that generated human speech using phonemes—bits of speech that form words when strung together. This same soundboard was used on Gottlieb's pinball games. And having used that chip before, Dave was aware of its unfortunate limitations. For one thing, the voice was monotone and not human-sounding at all. For another, it had a hard time with certain sounds. An attempt to have it say the word "bonus" inevitably resulted in it sounding like "bogus."

So, when presented with the task of creating a death sound for Q*bert (after a collision or a plummet off the pyramid), and having been frustrated by this chip in the past, Dave had a brilliant idea that was inspired to some extent by Jeff's comic swearing balloon. He decided to just throw random numbers at the Votrax and see what would happen. The result is the gibberish that became Q*bert's voice. In reality, it's just a bunch of random phonemes emitted as a single phrase. That means if you think you're hearing an actual word, it's possible that you are, however unlikely. As the theorem states, an infinite number of monkeys typing on an infinite number of typewriters will produce the entire works of William Shakespeare. In the case of Q*bert speaking words . . . most likely, you're imagining it.

The only words that Dave actually coded into the game are:

1) When the machine is powered on, you will hear "Hello, I'm turned on."

2) After you enter your initials into the high score table, you will hear "Bye-bye."

One of my favorite sounds that Dave created—and I believe it's used in all of Gottlieb's in-house games, both video and pinball—is the coin-drop sound. Dave managed to use our soundboard, which didn't have any capability to play sampled sounds, to algorithmically create the sound of a coin dropping into a metal box. It played whenever someone dropped a coin or token into a game's coin slot. It was so unexpectedly realistic, it always got a laugh from players upon hearing it for the first time.

MOVING TO NORTHLAKE

Sometime during the development of this game that was not yet called *Q*bert*, Gottlieb's upper management decided to move the video division from our relative isolation in the Bensenville plant to Gottlieb's main location in Northlake, about eight miles away. I'm not sure what the exact reasons were, but it made sense, I guess. The video division's first in-house game, *Reactor*, was about to be released. The department was growing and perhaps out-growing the available space at Bensenville. And of course it'd be easier for the suits to keep an eye on things if everyone were closer. The autonomy given to Ron and Howie in creating the video department would still be in place, but now that Tim Skelly's *Reactor* was about to roll off the production lines, other parts of the company, most notably manufacturing, needed to get involved.

Whatever the reasons, we showed up one day to our new home at 165 W. Lake Street. I don't recall the exact size of the video department, but I'd guess it had grown to well over twenty people. The space was much larger than what we'd had at Bensenville, with cubicles giving us at least the illusion of privacy. Surrounding the cubicles were offices for the managers and sound guys. Sound guys tended to make a lot of noise, so having them in offices with walls and doors made it easier for everyone else to do their jobs.

Naturally, there were people working there we'd never met. I recall being kind of excited about moving to the main plant, in part because we'd get to meet all of the pinball designers. Gottlieb's history as a pinball manufacturer was illustrious, and many of us video guys were pinball fans. I was looking forward to meeting the people who had created those games I loved playing.

Unfortunately, management didn't arrange any kind of mixer or meet-and-greet to prepare us or the Northlake employees for this merger of personnel. We arrived that first day, wide-eyed and stumbling about looking for our offices, to some friendly faces. But as we walked by other people, we would get the stink eye. You know, that subtle glance that says, "Go home. We don't want you here."

I was a little perplexed by this reaction. Being a friendly person in general, I always liked meeting new people, especially people I admired (like pinball designers). But I really didn't know what to make of this. Thankfully, it was subtle enough that it didn't affect my ability to settle in and get back to work.

What we newbies from the video department didn't know—and had no way of knowing, really—was that the pinball designers resented us from the start. The rise of video games was meteoric in the coin-op industry and had caused pinball to slip in popularity. Gottlieb was one of the last pinball companies to jump on the video bandwagon, and they chose to start their video division far from the main plant, which caused the pinball designers to feel a bit left out. I'm sure some of them would have liked to try their hand at designing a video game, but they weren't given that opportunity. And now the video division was coming in and taking over a huge piece of real estate in what used to be their turf. It seemed we were displacing them. So it's really no surprise that they harbored this resentment.

Eventually, though, as they got to know us and we

got to know them, they stopped seeing us as a personal threat to their livelihood and we all got along. It took a while, though. Gottlieb's upper management could have handled it a lot better.

One of the small advantages of our new location was having new places to go to lunch. I have very few recollections of where we ate lunch when we worked at Bensenville. That plant was in the middle of an industrial park behind O'Hare Airport, so there wasn't really any place to walk to. I'm pretty sure there was a White Castle we'd visit, but no other places come to mind. I always loved White Castle. If a group of us went to White Castle, we could eat enough burgers to stack the boxes into a pyramid. Hmm . . . could that have been the subconscious inspiration for my playfield?

Northlake provided us with more dining options. I have very fond memories of us going to lunch at the nearby Portillo's Hot Dogs and taking occasional trips to the Entenmann's Discount Bakery to bring some heavily discounted desserts back to the office. And even better, there was a White Castle within walking distance! Sometimes, it's the little things that bring a smile to your face.

Once we were settled in to our new home, I got back to work on the Cubes Game. All the elements were falling into place. At some point, I was given an arcade cabinet to house the monitor and electronics, along with a control panel to go with my diagonally mounted joystick. Now, when people in the office came by to play it, the experience was closer to what it would be in an arcade. Finally, I could stop explaining to people why they shouldn't rotate the joystick bucket. Yet I *still* got numerous requests to straighten the damn thing! Some people just couldn't break out of the habit of pushing a joystick up and down, or right and left. This annoyed and confused me because it seemed pretty obvious that the diagonal orientation was the only natural choice for this playfield. Despite the many complaints, I stuck to my guns on this, mostly because I had no backup plan. Making a player jump straight up and down or left and right meant creating an entirely different playfield and rewriting virtually all of my motion-related code. Wasn't gonna happen.

Some time after the move to Northlake, our development systems were replaced. As more programmers were hired, it became clear that sharing Blue Boxes wasn't going to work anymore. Buying new ones made no sense because they were expensive and becoming outdated. A newer machine was available that was cheaper and extensible—meaning it could do much more than just serving as our development system. Part of that extensibility was a card slot cage that allowed you to plug in circuit boards for any purpose you needed. This miraculous device was the IBM PC, first introduced in 1981.

Not only could the IBM PC take the place of a Blue Box—via an In-Circuit Emulator board that fit into one of the PC's internal card slots—it also had a variety of other valuable functions. It could act as a word processor for documents and, with the appropriate software and circuit board, an EEPROM burner. EEPROM is an acronym for "Electrically Erasable Programmable Read-Only Memory," which is simply an integrated circuit chip that could hold data. Unlike a regular ROM, though, EEPROMs were reusable through a process called "burning," which just meant over-writing. We stored our image and program data in EEPROMs, since those would change frequently during the development and testing of a game. Once the game was officially released, ROMs (which could not be re-written) would be used in those slots.

Those first IBM PCs had two floppy disk drives and no hard disks. The original floppy drives took 5 ¼-inch

Creating Q*bert

single-sided disks that held 180 kilobytes of data each. Just to give you a perspective, 1 kilobyte = 1,024 bytes; 1 megabyte = 1,024 x 1,024 bytes; and 1 gigabyte = 1,024 x 1,024 x 1,024 bytes. By the time Gottlieb bought PCs for development, double-sided disks were available, which held 360 kilobytes. This was more than enough for our needs. Our games only had 64 kilobytes of program memory, 64 kilobytes for foreground images (sprites), and 32 kilobytes for background blocks. When the first hard disks came out a few months later, their 1-megabyte capacity seemed like more memory than we could possibly ever need!

TUNING

Tuning is one of the most daunting aspects of video game design, and arcade games require a special kind of tuning since they are supposed to be quarter-suckers for the people that own them. It's important to understand that Gottlieb's role in this business was as a manufacturer. They built the game and made their money from selling the actual machines to a distributor, not from what was put into the coin box after the game reached its location. The distributors sold the games to arcade operators (or bar owners, pizza places, etc.), or they might split the coin box intake with certain locations. However, if a game didn't collect enough quarters, it wouldn't appeal to the distributors, and they wouldn't buy as many—which in turn meant the manufacturer wouldn't build as many.

I certainly didn't consider myself an "artist" in my game-making career, but I also wasn't a crass capitalist whose goal was to bilk the public out of their quarters. I did, however, have to serve two masters if possible. My game had to be fun and entertaining (to please my audience, which included me), and it had to earn money (to please management). So proper tuning was actually a huge part of the job. And I'd never done it before! This presented a major challenge. How fast should each object move? How much should speeds change from level to level? When would enemies be released, and how often? How would one level differ from the next? Questions were many, and answers were all yet to be determined.

The first step in tuning is to have people who've never played the game play it. And watch them. This had been going on from the very beginning with my fellow employees. But the size of the group in Bensenville was relatively small, and the game was no longer new to them. After the move to Northlake, I had a nice new sampling of people: some avid game players (and some not so much) who might wander by (or be dragged over) to play.

Exposing the game to a new populace also meant new suggestions. Everybody had an opinion of what would make the game better. "Oh, you should have him do . . ." this or that or whatever. I already mentioned the grief I got about the joystick. As always, I politely took in all suggestions, and in the rare case that one grabbed me, I implemented it. A very popular suggestion among new players was to prevent the player from plummeting off the pyramid, which usually came right after they did exactly that. But most people managed to learn to stay on the pyramid after a couple of tries, so it seemed a reasonable skill to ask of them. Something else I heard a lot was that everything moved too fast. I heard this complaint so often, I felt the need to respond, so I dialed back the speed of every object at the start of the game. Even after this adjustment, I got the same complaint, so I tweaked it some more.

There was one other significant suggestion that I gladly took. Rick Tighe, one of our engineering techs, was playing the game one day and said, "You know what would be great?" (Of course, most suggestions started that way, but this time it was true.) "What if when he fell, we put a pinball knocker in the bottom of the cabinet and knocked it, like he landed at the bottom?"

A genius idea, although I did have one variation to add. A pinball knocker makes a hard sound, like knuckles on a wood door. But I wanted to hear a sound more like a sack of potatoes hitting the ground. A thud. We came up with a solution of placing just a tiny bit of foam rubber on the cabinet where the knocker struck to soften the sound a bit. I wrote the code to trigger the knocker at the proper time, and . . . magic! It sounded perfect. It drew the reality of the game off the screen and into the real world in a very fun way, and I loved that. It also got the seal of approval from everyone who heard and felt it.

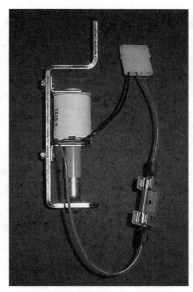

This is the knocker that was mounted at the bottom of each *Q*bert* cabinet. Normally used for pinball machines, it has a piston that shoots out and knocks on the side of the cabinet. A dip switch on the circuit board could enable or disable it.

The only problem was that the addition of that piece of foam was deemed too labor-intensive for the production line, and was scrapped. I recall being told that it would add fifteen dollars to the cost of each game built to add the foam, and management thought that was too much. I was severely disappointed. When the game finally went into production, it was shipped with no foam, and with the knocker feature as a dip-switch setting so arcade owners could turn it off if they wanted. (And many did; it was loud and, in some environments, annoying.) But it became one of the most unique and beloved features of the game. And ever since, I've had to live with the knowledge of just how much better it could have been.

A big part of tuning is trying to engage and entertain the casual player who might only last through the first couple of levels, while still challenging the more expert players. The problem, though, is that there were no expert players while I was coding the game! I certainly wasn't one. And although some Gottlieb employees were better than me, I really couldn't foresee just how good some players would become. Not that I didn't try.

Somewhere in this paragraph is a piece of secret information. For those of you who are not familiar with *Q*bert*, there are four "rounds" in each level. Every round has a target color for the cube tops. The game gets slightly faster with each round, and when you advance to a new level, there are some wrinkles to the basic gameplay that I added. In the first level of the game, you just have to jump on a cube once to change it to the target color. For Level 2, it takes two jumps. In Level 3, it only takes one jump, but if you jump on that cube again, it changes back to the original color. And so on, for two more levels. Each level is numbered, and they increase up until Level 9. If you're good enough to last that long, subsequent levels are all labeled "9." But the dirty little secret of *Q*bert* is that the tuning actually doesn't change after Level 5.

That's right—Levels 6 through 9 and beyond are all simply re-using the same tuning tables for Level 5. The reason for this was simple: I didn't think anyone would ever play that far on one quarter! That's also the reason the level number never goes higher than "9." The graphic only had room for one digit, and it didn't seem worth it to create another one, since no one was expected to reach Level 9.

It's kind of funny. I've read over the years in certain articles or books that *Q*bert* was designed by committee. Or some variation on that, which implies that I played a minor role in its development. This is simply untrue. Of all the games I've worked on in my career, *Q*bert* is probably the one for which I can take the most ownership. Because with the exception of some utility routines provided to me by Tim Skelly, I wrote every line of code in that game, and as the project's designated designer I made every decision as to what went into that game and what did not. Even Jeff Lee, who is often credited as co-designer (and I don't begrudge him that title, because he created all of the characters and was my trusted collaborator and sounding board), didn't have the ability to ensure that any idea would be implemented. Just because I was inexperienced didn't mean I wasn't in control of the game's design. I was guided, for better or worse, by my instincts as a game player and my personal taste.

Before I began working at Gottlieb, I'd read something Steven Spielberg said about one of his movies (it might have been *Jaws*), and it stayed with me. In essence, he said he set out to make a movie that he himself would like to see. That's how I felt about video games. I wanted to please the player in me, in the hope that there were other players out there who would appreciate it as much as I did. I tried to do that with *Q*bert*—and after I had exhausted my available pool of in-house testers and finally felt that the game was ready to be unleashed on the world, I was nervous to learn whether or not I'd succeeded.

CHAPTER FOUR

A NOSER IS BORN

The Cubes Game was pretty much complete. I'd programmed as many gameplay elements as I wanted to, and tuned it as much as possible based on observations and feedback from Gottlieb's employees. Now it needed what I'd avoided giving it from the start: a proper name. I thought I was pretty dispassionate about whatever name the game would ultimately have. To me, the game itself was the accomplishment. I figured that if it was good, whatever we called it would stick in people's minds. It didn't take long for that notion to be tested.

Everyone at Gottlieb seemed to agree that the player character's charm was one of the game's greatest strengths. His look, the way he moved, the way he spoke, his plight, all worked together to create empathy for him. And so it was agreed that the name of the game should be the name of the character. Before that decision, I distinctly remember the phrase "Why me?" being suggested as a name. I'm pretty sure that was a Howie Rubin suggestion. Howie was definitely an out-of-the-box thinker.

Howie also wanted to call the game "@!#?@!" That's right. Howie wanted the game's name to be the unpronounceable contents of the cartoon balloon cursing when the player gets killed. And he was more serious about that than his "Why me?" idea.

"But Howie," I asked him, "what will people call it?"

Howie, smiling, made a gibberish sound.

"That's insane!" said the echoing unified voice of everyone who had heard this idea.

Howie was grinning like an inspired madman. "That's why it's going to work! If the game is good enough—and it is—people will find a way to talk about it."

We all tried to talk some sense into Howie. I appreciated the boldness of his concept, but it just seemed completely impractical. Howie, though, never let go of the idea, and a number of marquees were later created for testing with the cartoon swearing as the name of the game.

Being the democratic kind of person that I was, and knowing that many people at Gottlieb liked to make suggestions, I decided to poll everyone in the office and ask them what they thought the name of the character should be. I wrote all the suggestions down on a pad as I collected them, and oh how I wish I still had that piece of paper. Two columns of twenty-six lines were all filled as I polled programmers, artists, sound guys, hardware designers, pinball designers, technicians, middle managers, secretaries, and anyone else who wanted to contribute. Sadly, the only contribution I remember was by Frank Starshak, one of our managers, who suggested Arnie Aardvark. I believe it was the long nose that inspired this suggestion. And I mean no insult to Frank, but what I felt towards this name was the same as I felt toward every other name I'd written down on that paper. It was terrible. I realized I was not as dispassionate about the name as I'd thought.

So with no tangible name and a pressing need to come up with one, we decided to have a meeting. Jeff and I were there, along with Howie and Ron. Dave Thiel was not, although I'm not sure why. Also in attendance were art director Rich Tracy, marketing manager Dave Berte, managers Bill Jacobs and Frank Starshak, and possibly a few others I've forgotten. The meeting began and everyone offered up ideas for the name of the game and the character. We discussed the names on the list, with people picking their favorites and arguing for some and against others. I didn't really have anything to offer—I was just waiting for something to sound palatable. So I just took everything in. I'm not positive about this, but I think I may have been the youngest person in the room. And at some point I had an out-of-body experience. The ridiculousness of these grown men throwing out the most childish-sounding cartoon names and discussing their merits and drawbacks with utter seriousness struck me as just too absurd. I felt like I was in a Monty Python sketch.

After some number of hours, with everyone tired and worn down and still with no actual name to walk away with, someone walked over to the whiteboard and wrote the name HUBERT. At this point, I can't remember with absolute certainty who did what.

"Why Hubert?" we all asked.

"Well, it's a name. And it seems to suit the character. Plus it sounds like 'cube' and the game is about cubes."

There was some grumbling in the room. It was like we'd been here before. Then someone else walked up and replaced the "H" with a "C."

"Well, what if it was Cubert?"

Everyone perked up. Somehow we all felt we were on to something. I've always attributed this next part to Rich Tracy, though in fairness, I'm not sure who it was that walked up and replaced the "CU" with "Q-."

"How about this . . . Q-bert?"

You could literally feel the energy in the room growing. This was getting exciting. No one was nay-saying. There were only nods and smiles and expressions of approval.

Creating Q*bert

Jeff Lee added the final touch, changing the dash into an asterisk. In my mind's dramatic recreation of the scene, everyone rose to their feet, shouting and cheering, hugging one another and crying. But I'm sure that was mostly internal. Still, everyone miraculously was in agreement. The game and the character had a name: Q*bert.

And thanks to Tim Skelly he would soon have a nickname, inspired by the Canadian sketch comedy show *Second City Television*, which had started airing on U.S. television in 1981. A regular feature on *Second City TV* was Dave Thomas and Rick Moranis playing Bob and Doug McKenzie, two fictional brothers who, in thick Canadian accents, popularized the catchphrase "Hey, you hoser!"

I'm not sure when, but at some point while Tim Skelly was watching Q*bert being played in our offices, he casually called out, "Hey, you noser!" Everybody in the room laughed and not only did it catch on, but I added it to the game. The high score initial entry page proudly proclaims: "Welcome to the Noser Elite!" And the player claiming the highest score would earn the title of "Supreme Noser."

FIELD-TESTING

Before Q*bert could be field-tested—that is, put into a cabinet and placed in an actual arcade—it needed some artwork. Not the pixelated kind, but rather something to adorn the cabinet. This work was done by Terry Doerzaph, a talented graphic artist and cabinet designer who to my knowledge never worked on video graphics, only cabinet and promotional art. Some of his work on Q*bert exists today in the form of hand-drawn preliminary cabinet art, which went out on test before the assembly line was set up for an actual production run. Maybe a dozen or so "engineering samples," as we called them, were put together for testing. The preliminary art on the marquee and control panel differed slightly from what was to appear on production cabinets, and the sides of the engineering samples displayed a generic pattern, rather than Terry's *Q*bert*-specific side art.

At Howie's insistence, some cabinets went out with the marquee featuring the swearing cartoon balloon. Even the control panel displayed "@!#?@!" as the name of the game, although the box labeled "Who's Who and What's What" correctly identified the player character as Q*bert. The game's antagonists all appeared in that same box. Jeff named them all with my blessing. Coily was an obvious choice for our coiled snake nemesis. The names Slick and Sam, given to the green creatures who worked against the player by turning cubes back from their target color, was a play on the phrase "spick-and-span." Slick wore the shades, and Sam was named for programmer Sam Russo. Not sure where Ugg's name came from, but for the other enemy whose gravity was aligned to the cube's side rather than its top, Wrong-Way was right on the nose.

Field-testing was a standard practice among arcade game manufacturers. Before committing to buying these expensive machines, distributors wanted to have some sense of whether or not they'd make a profit or at least recoup their cost. Remember, manufacturers like Gottlieb, Stern, and Williams just built the machines and made their money by selling them. Their customers were by and large distributors—basically middle-men who either sold the games to arcade owners or had arrangements to place them at locations for a cut of the coin collections. For a distributor to place a large order for a particular game, they'd want to know that it had value. It was all

Creating Q*bert

well and good if a game had nice graphics or innovative gameplay, but to distributors, value meant the ability to collect quarters, hopefully for a long time. So manufacturers would put their games out into the real world and conduct "coin tests" for a few weeks to gauge player interest, and use the collected coin data to (hopefully) get distributors interested.

A few locations in the Chicago area had an arrangement with Gottlieb. We would put a new game at their location and they would report the coins collected each week, and in exchange they'd get to keep those coins. Some locations might be arcades, others might be bars or bowling alleys. It was a great system, with the added bonus that I could go to these public locations and watch people play the game. The first time I watched *Q*bert* being played outside of Gottlieb's walls, I wasn't sure exactly what I was looking for—this was a new experience for me—but I knew that watching "real" people play (not just the folks at Gottlieb) would be helpful.

I have some very clear memories of watching the game being played at one particular arcade. It was fascinating. The cabinet was wheeled into a nice spot near the center of the arcade. I hung back, trying not to be conspicuous and also trying not to seem like some crazy predator. I was nervous. I wanted people to like the game, but this was 1982, at the height of the arcade industry. A lot of new games were coming out, so I was concerned about competition.

A few people walked by *Q*bert* and looked at it—just a glance—then kept walking. Some people stopped and watched the "attract mode" (a term for what appears on the screen when the game isn't being played), then moved on after a while. Some people who'd walked away before came back to look at it again. It was kind of nerve-racking. When was someone going to actually try to play it?

Eventually, it happened. It was a child—a girl, maybe eight years old. She put a quarter in, waited for the game to start, and immediately jumped off the pyramid to her death. I started sweating. I hoped she'd learn from her mistake on her next life, but before I could finish that thought, she did the exact same thing. I wanted to go to her and help her understand what she was doing wrong, but that wouldn't be very scientific. I needed to just be an observer. I watched in horror as she jumped off the playfield a third time and died yet again, using up her final life and ending the game. She walked away. Her entire game had lasted around thirty seconds.

The memory of people at Gottlieb telling me the game was too hard crept into my brain. People had specifically told me it was a bad idea to allow the player to jump off the playfield. Should I have listened? I'd stuck to my guns on that one, just like I had with the 45-degree angled joystick. Was I wrong?

This was not a very auspicious start, but I rationalized that she was young. Maybe an older player would get the hang of it sooner. I waited a while longer and then another brave soul—this time a boy, maybe twelve—watched the screen a bit before popping in a quarter. He managed to move around the playfield successfully before getting clobbered by a ball. His next two lives ended pretty much the same. His quarter spent, he walked away.

And so it went with the next few people who came by. They'd give it a shot, achieve varying degrees of success, then move on after playing one game. I envisioned a bleak future for myself. Maybe I just wasn't cut out to make video games.

And then something surprising happened. The little girl, the first one who'd only managed to fall off the pyramid, came back. She watched someone else play Q*bert.

When they left, she put in another quarter and played again, this time staying on the playfield and lasting a bit longer. Other players who'd left came back, too. Like the girl, they watched someone else play for a while, learning from someone else's mistakes before trying again and doing better on their second attempts. Some even stayed for another game or two.

This was remarkable! People seemed challenged by the game, but were sticking with it! I breathed a huge sigh of relief and tried to learn something useful as I watched players' reactions. I'm not sure how many hours I spent in observation that first day, but I tried very hard not to make any knee-jerk decisions based on this relatively small sample of players. Yet it seemed pretty obvious that the game was still too hard for beginners. I went back to work and continued to tweak, making it slower and easier in those first levels.

FOCUS GROUPS

Another method that Gottlieb used to obtain feedback on *Q*bert* before its release was focus groups. If you've never been on a focus group, it's basically a dozen or so people chosen randomly from some public place who are paid a small fee in exchange for trying out a product and then giving their impressions and opinions. Our Market Research Director, Dave Berte, and his assistant, Jean, ran Gottlieb's focus groups.

I remember some of the attendees of *Q*bert*'s focus group being kids, or at least teenagers who had come with their parents. They arrived at some office (not Gottlieb's offices, I recall) and were escorted to a conference room with a *Q*bert* cabinet in the corner and a large mirror on one wall. This, of course, was a one-way mirror, on the other side of which sat myself and some of Gottlieb's managers, watching and listening to everything that went on.

Either Dave or Jean addressed the attendees, explaining to them how important their opinions were and assuring them that they could speak freely and honestly whether their impressions were positive or negative. Then everyone got a chance to play the game for a while.

Watching this unfold was even more surreal than watching the game being played in an arcade. First of all, there was a sense of artificiality about it. Let's face it, a conference room does not have the same vibe as an arcade. Everyone playing games in an arcade is there to do just that, while the focus group consisted of people whose intention was to go to the mall. Not all of the participants were "video game players." They might never have played Q*bert, had they come across it on their own. So while some people took to the game pretty quickly, just as might happen in an arcade, others had a hard time. But watching them all play was absolutely fascinating, seeing their faces betray frustration at falling off the playfield or getting killed by a bouncing ball or having their progress undone by Slick and Sam. Seeing triumph as they narrowly avoided Ugg or Wrong-Way or evaded Coily by jumping onto a disk. If nothing else, I realized that, by some miracle, the game was working.

After the gameplay portion ended, the questions and discussion began. What did you like about the game? What did you not like about the game? Would you pay to play this game in an arcade? Which character did you like the best? Which did you like the least? What part of the game was too hard? And so on.

A lot of the usual things came up: "Why is the joystick diagonal?" "It's too easy to jump off the pyramid and die." Some things were new: "I don't like the colors."

One was particularly weird: "It looked like the screen inverted." This was a comment I'd heard every now and then after the game was released. Apparently when some people look at the playfield, their brains process the Escher illusion in such a way that the cubes look upside down. My response to this was the same as for the other usual criticisms:

"Um, okay."

As for the pyramid, the joystick, and the risk of falling to your death, there really wasn't anything I felt I could do to fix those things, short of creating a new game from scratch.

During the group discussion, I noticed a phenomenon that kind of surprised me. There were people who clearly enjoyed the game while they were playing it. I'd seen it in their faces and body language. But then during the Q&A, some of their answers seemed to contradict their behavior. They claimed they didn't enjoy it, said it didn't engage them even though I had clearly seen otherwise. This taught me a valuable lesson about human behavior. People, when given the opportunity to criticize, will find things to criticize. And behavior speaks louder than words.

What I learned from the focus groups was that there really wasn't much to change except for making the game slower and easier, which I reluctantly did once again. Honestly, I felt I'd tuned the game to be so easy at the beginning that I really couldn't slow it down any more, or it would seem to be slow motion. I can't say that I experienced any pressure from management to make any changes. Howie and Ron weren't shy about letting me know if they disagreed with me, but they never ordered me to change anything. They supported every decision I made.

Seriously, I can't praise those two guys enough.

Although there was one time when even their considerable influence couldn't help me.

In the last few weeks of developing and tweaking, I worked a lot of overtime, including weekends. I wanted to make sure every aspect of the game was behaving as it should and playing the way I wanted it to. I had clearance to enter the building 24/7, and weekends tended to be pretty quiet since the building was all but deserted. The only problem was that it was freezing! Despite a hot Chicago summer, it was absurdly cold inside the offices on the weekends. I don't know why, but the air conditioning was cranked up to the point where, after a couple of hours of typing, I could no longer feel my fingers and I'd have to step outside to let the sun warm up my hands. I asked Howie and Ron if they could do something about it, but despite their powers, which included protecting us from the goings-on in upper management, they were apparently at the mercy of whoever controlled the thermostat.

PRODUCTION

As *Q*bert* got closer to production, some design decisions needed to be made about its cabinet. I was no expert on this subject, but as a game player, I had opinions. Those at Gottlieb who were responsible for cabinet design had learned a few things from their few prior attempts. The licensed games *New York! New York!* and *No Man's Land* had cabinets so generic, I'm not even sure if any "design" went into them. Our first in-house game, Tim Skelly's *Reactor*, had a cabinet designed with Tim's input, based on his experience with the games he'd created for Cinematronics.

Concerning *Q*bert*'s cabinet design, I remember conversations about every possible detail, from the cabinet's height to the angle of the monitor and the slope of the control panel. They wanted a sloping control panel rather than a level one, so people wouldn't set their drinks on it. But it was also common for people in arcades to place quarters on the control panel to reserve the next game, and so we needed the panel to have a lip to keep quarters from sliding off.

Another concern was glare from overhead light, which could become a problem depending on the angle of the monitor and the bezel in front of it. All manufacturers tried varying solutions to these issues, and Gottlieb was no exception. *Reactor*'s cabinet didn't do much to reduce glare. For *Q*bert*, the marquee was extended a bit to provide some cover for the monitor.

In addition to the standard upright cabinet, Gottlieb produced a number of tabletop cabinets, which were called "cocktail" cabinets because they were primarily intended for bars. The cabinet looked liked a glass-covered table, with the monitor facing directly upwards. A player would sit in a chair to play. For two player games, the players would sit opposite each other and the screen would flip upside down between players' turns. Jun Yum included a feature in our hardware to allow this, and my software had to flip the screen at the appropriate time. Rather than have a whole new set of program ROMs for cocktail tables, the feature was selectable by a dip switch on our circuit board.

By October of 1982, *Q*bert* was getting ready to roll off the production line, which was winding down from building Tim Skelly's *Reactor*. That game, though innovative in gameplay and popular among some hard-core players, didn't sell as many units as management had hoped. And without another game to build, Gottlieb would have to lay people off or slow down the production line's output, which they really hoped to avoid. The pinball industry had gone through many cycles of feast or famine, and the companies that survived got used to dealing with these fluctuations. (It's likely that a slowdown in pinball sales was part of the reason Gottlieb decided to get into the video game business in the first place.) But unlike pinball, the video game industry was thriving and Gottlieb needed a hit to justify their investment in video to their parent company, Columbia Pictures, which had recently been purchased by Coca-Cola. *Q*bert* arrived just in time to keep the production line going, and management hoped they'd get enough orders to keep the line moving as close to full capacity as possible.

Mind you, I felt none of the pressure or apprehension that management felt as *Reactor* ended its run. I was blissfully ignorant to matters of business. I was hired to make video games, and I'd made one. I was floating on a cloud of satisfaction.

Q*bert officially debuted in November of 1982 during one of the coin-op industry's big trade shows, sponsored by the Amusement Machine Operators Association (AMOA). The basic tone of a typical AMOA show was kind of like an amusement park. The booths were big and lavish, colorful with lots of lights, designed to draw you in. Manufacturers showed off their latest and greatest pinball machines, video games, shuffle alleys, redemption games, vending machines, jukeboxes, and anything else designed for the ultimate purpose of collecting coins. If you've ever attended or seen video of a modern E3 or CES, you'll get the idea.

And, of course, there were booth babes. (I didn't make up the name—that's what they were, and largely still are, called.) I'm referring of course to the beautiful women (usually wearing skimpy or form-fitting costumes) who were hired to stand at a manufacturer's booth and hand out flyers. The women Gottlieb hired tended to be dressed more conservatively than some others. This practice continues at trade shows to this day, though I'd like to believe they're treated with more respect now. Back then, it wasn't uncommon to see men leering at booth babes, asking them for dates or trying to get them to come to some party.

That year, at my first AMOA, it was quite a thrill seeing a line of *Q*bert* games set on free play, surrounded by crowds of people enthusiastically playing. Meanwhile, Gottlieb's sales force was there to do business, sharing earnings reports and trying to convince buyers that *Q*bert* was the best game to order at the show. After all, it had a lot going for it. It looked unlike anything else out there, it had a small buzz locally from players who'd seen it on test, and it had coin test data that showed it to be a strong earner. At the end of the day, we did pretty well. Management seemed pleased, and some people called *Q*bert* the "game of the show."

Orders poured in and *Q*bert* machines started rolling off our production line. Looking back, I wish I'd taken more of an interest in the manufacturing side of our industry. I had virtually no involvement with it. Even when I was told that putting a small piece of foam on the cabinet where the knocker would hit was too "labor-intensive," it was conveyed to me second-hand. I don't recall ever interacting with anyone from manufacturing. But I did get to go down to the plant to watch *Q*bert* arcade machines being built. It's hard to convey the feeling of seeing cabinet after cabinet in a row being assembled, and knowing that everyone there has a job because of what Jeff, Dave, and I did. I'm not sure how many *Q*bert* machines were built every day, but it was enough to keep the plant busy for a few months.

As 1982 came to a close, *Q*bert* cabinets slowly infiltrated the market. We shipped them to distributors, who in turn placed them in arcades, bars, bowling alleys, pizza joints, and convenience stores. Once the ROMs (the memory chips that stored the program and images) were finalized, there was nothing left for me to do. It felt like an eternity with no feedback, no goal, and lots of time on my hands. I started to worry about my tweaks and tuning.

"What if I made it *too* slow?"

"What if I made it *too* easy?"

I had worked so hard to avoid discouraging new players, but would advanced players become bored with those easy first levels? My inexperience felt like a huge burden.

Within a few weeks, reports filtered in about some people playing the game for hours on one quarter. *One* quarter! My worst fears had been realized! It didn't matter that these reports were rare. It bothered me that *anyone* would be able to play to Level 5 on one quarter. If they could get that far, they could probably play indefinitely! Obviously, a game that can be played for hours on one quarter doesn't take in as much money as one with lots of turnaround, and if an operator has a game that's not taking in money, they're going to want to replace it with a better earner as soon as possible. I panicked, thinking if I didn't take immediate action the game would die a quick death. I felt so stupid to have so severely underestimated the abilities of the players out in the real world.

FHMC Q*BERT

Since the game was technically finished and released, there was little to no chance of distributing new ROMs into the field. But I kept tinkering with it because . . . well . . . just in case? In all honesty, I was doing it for my own mental well-being. I got Jeff involved and we had discussions about how to make an advanced version of the game.

Some changes were no-brainers. Speed up the game from the start. Restructure the levels to be harder to complete. Other changes were made based on ideas we had once the game was on test and basically finalized, such as having the disks move up the pyramid so you had to time your jumps to land on them, and adding a bonus round to give the player a breather while they racked up some points (and perhaps an extra life). Another was adding levels where Slick and Sam, who usually changed cubes back to a previous color, now changed them to a never-before-seen pattern that Q*bert couldn't affect. These patterns could only be changed by Coily or a new enemy we had created: Q*bertha, a female counterpart of Q*bert who moved and behaved pretty much like Coily. This forced the player to lead his pursuer over the affected cubes.

I was really loving this new game, whatever it was. It wasn't really a sequel, but it felt like more than just a re-tuning. Howie and Ron knew I was working on it, but they didn't really know what to do with it. *Q*bert* was still on its initial production run, and as it appeared in more locations across the country, word about it was spreading. Operators and distributors seemed to be happy, orders kept coming in, and the game seemed to be collecting pretty well, as far as we heard. So there really was no need for this new version.

I used to frequent a bar in Chicago called the Gaslight Corner. It was an actor hangout, next door to the Lois Hall Studio, where I took acting classes at night. The Gaslight had a few arcade games in the back and, lo and behold, one day a *Q*bert* appeared. I couldn't believe it! It was extremely surreal, watching people play my game in "my" bar. I had to fight the urge to tell everyone playing it that I created it. Maybe that sounds weird, but here was my thinking. First of all, why should they believe me? I couldn't prove such an outrageous claim. And second, what did I expect them to do in response? Hoist me up on their shoulders and sing "For He's a Jolly Good Fellow?" Of course not! Besides, by then I'd gotten used to lurking behind people and just watching them play while I quietly enjoyed a sense of pride. I was fine to keep doing that.

But every time I saw someone master the game and play through to Level 5 or beyond, I felt a knot in my stomach. I really wanted to see how my souped-up, improved version would play to the masses. My pitch to management was that at some point, people were going to master the current version of *Q*bert* and become bored with it. Why not have an advanced replacement ready and waiting in the wings? Since the new version didn't require any changes to our hardware or sounds, we could release it as a kit so current *Q*bert* owners could upgrade without having to buy a whole new machine. The kit would consist of new foreground, background, and program ROMs, along with a new marquee and maybe a new overlay for the control panel. For a relatively small cost, distributors would have a new(ish) game with a longer shelf life. And who knows? If the new version became really popular, maybe then we could build more dedicated cabinets.

Of course, this enhanced version needed a name. I thought of obvious things like *Q*bert 2* and *Super Q*bert*, but those didn't appeal to me. Whenever someone at work asked me what made the new game different from the old one, my answer was, "Well, it's faster. It's harder. And it's more challenging." I said that so often, it eventually struck me that it would make the perfect name: *Faster, Harder, More Challenging Q*bert*, or *FHMC Q*bert* for short.

Once I finished *FHMC Q*bert*, Howie and Ron wanted to put it out on test. I was all for it, having convinced myself that players were bored with the original and would welcome this new challenge. But that wasn't the case, and coin returns after field-testing *FHMC Q*bert* for a couple of weeks were low. Apparently, only a relatively small number of gamers were getting to *Q*bert*'s highest levels, while the majority were still getting the hang of it. People weren't looking for a version that was more difficult. Coin collections for the original were still strong, and didn't warrant releasing the new version, so management scrapped it. Why they didn't just wait a year and release it then is a mystery to me to this day. But *FHMC Q*bert* would return someday. We'll get to that later.

One interesting thing about *FHMC Q*bert* that has nothing to do with gameplay is that it became part of an attempt by Gottlieb to fight overseas piracy. At the time, the Chinese were very adept at making knockoff boards that would run American games, and there was a healthy black market for counterfeit games in Asia. American video manufacturers were trying to figure out ways to fight it. When Gottlieb put *FHMC Q*bert* on test, its ROMs were attached to a small circuit board that scrambled the signals coming out of them, and the whole thing was dipped into a resin that hardened into a brick-like block. You'd have to plug this brick into a socket on our hardware to unscramble the signals correctly so the game could run. Seemed like a good idea, but I don't think it was ever used on any other game.

SOME ANONYMOUS PUBLICITY

While I kept myself busy with *FHMC Q*bert*, the original *Q*bert* continued to infiltrate the United States (and

Play Meter's Picks

Q*Bert heads the list as *Play Meter*'s in-house choice for top game of the AMOA show. Publisher and Editor Ralph Lally II, Editorial Director David Pierson, and Mr. Player (a noted, anonymous expert) selected their top 10 games and those results were tabulated for a consensus list:

1. *Q*Bert* (Gottlieb)
2. *Popeye* (Nintendo)
3. *Super Pac-Man* (Bally)
4. *Buck Rogers* (Sega)
5. *Pole Position* (Atari)
6. *Burger Time* (Data East/Bally)
7. *Time Pilot* (Centuri)
8. *Baby Pac-Man* (Bally)
9. *Front Line* (Taito)
10. *Millipede* (Atari)
    tie
    Nibbler (Rock-Ola)

(Games like Sega's *Pengo*, Williams' *Joust*, and Nintendo's *Donkey Kong Junior*, etc., etc., etc., were not included in the rankings because they were introduced before the AMOA Show.)

How reliable are these selections? Look back in your January 1, 1982 *Play Meter*, page 24. Our top picks for AMOA 1981 were *Tempest, Qix, Donkey Kong, Galaga,* and *Frogger*. We aren't ones to brag, but these games fared well in the *Play Meter* Equipment Polls. (For further reference, see the top rankings of videos of 1982 on page 65 in the November 15 issue.)

All five of *Play Meter*'s consensus picks finished in the Top Performing Videos of 1982. In fact, of all the games released at the '81 AMOA show, only six (*Donkey Kong, Galaga, Stargate, Tempest, Qix,* and *Frogger* in that order) made it in the top 13 games of the year listing. The other top videos were either released prior to the '81 AMOA or later in 1982.

As far as the accuracy of our "experts" goes, Pierson was in front with five of five, Lally was a close second with four of five, and independent reviewers Roger Sharpe and Mike Bucki were in running distance with three out of five.

Nail this page to a door, and see how our experts finish with these games. By the end of the year, this page will be riddled with holes; or you'll have a bull's-eye! •

Lally	Pierson	Mr. Player
1. *Q*Bert*	1. *Q*Bert*	1. *Q*Bert*
2. *Popeye*	2. *Popeye*	2. *Super Pac-Man*
3. *Super Pac-Man*	3. *Baby Pac-Man*	3. *Buck Rogers*
4. *Buck Rogers*	4. *Time Pilot*	4. *Popeye*
5. *Burger Time*	5. *Front Line*	5. *Pole Position*
6. *Nibbler*	6. *Pole Position*	6. *Millipede*
7. *Time Pilot*	7. *Burger Time*	7. *Burger Time*
8. *Pole Position*	8. *Buck Rogers*	8. *Liberator*
9. *Front Line*	9. *Super Pac-Man*	9. *Time Pilot*
10. *Mr. F. Lea*	10. *Sinistar*	10. *Baby Pac-Man*

From industry magazine *Play Meter* January 15, 1983, a recap of their choices for best game of the AMOA 1982 show.

Europe, although I don't remember ever hearing much about its reception there). By early 1983, magazines such as *Electronic Gaming Monthly, Vidiot, Electronic Fun with Computers & Games,* and *JoyStik* all featured articles about *Q*bert*, many with mentions on the cover. And everything they said was good! I didn't know what to make of all the praise for the game. It was nice, but it didn't have an immediate impact on my life. Publicly, no one knew the names of the people responsible for *Q*bert*, as it was Gottlieb's policy to prohibit creator credits in any game. Tim Skelly, being under a contract with his own stipulations, was a notable exception. The rest of us were just lowly employees.

Although I wasn't aware of it at the time, apparently it was pretty common for companies to try to poach talent from their competitors. Gottlieb's management felt that if no one knew who made a game, other companies wouldn't know who to poach. Those of us at Gottlieb who were making games weren't thrilled with this policy, but I couldn't be too bothered by it, either. After all, I was happy just having the opportunity to make video games! I wasn't in it for the glory. But although fame was never a goal for me, it seemed fair and right to be recognized for something I'd done.

Then, writer Neil Tesser of *Video Games Magazine* wanted to do a cover article spotlighting *Q*bert* and *Joust*, two American-made video game successes recently unveiled at the previous AMOA show to a market where most of the huge hits were Japanese. *Joust* was made by Williams, another old pinball company which had entered the video game market to great success with *Defender*, *Stargate*, and *Robotron*.

Although I was considered *Q*bert's* project leader and designer, I really felt that Jeff's contributions to character design and gameplay and Dave's sound contributions were equally worthy of recognition. I thought of us as the *Q*bert* triumvirate, the creative team behind the game. When the request from *Video Games Magazine* came in, I insisted that we all be present for the interview. Gottlieb agreed, on the condition that none of our names be revealed in the article.

So one day, Neil Tesser came to our offices and Jeff Lee, Dave Thiel, and I sat down with him in a conference room to talk about the creation of *Q*bert*. When the article came out, we discovered that our pseudonyms were R. Teeste, J. Walkman, and D. Ziner. We all felt the cloak-and-dagger routine was a bit much, but we really had no choice in the matter. And it seemed even crazier and sillier when we saw that Williams had no problem acknowledging John Newcomer as the creator of *Joust*!

I know management took a lot of flak over that *Video Games* article, and some of it came from me. It became hard to justify keeping their game creators under wraps when one of their most successful competitors had no problem allowing their people credit. Shortly after, management relaxed enough to let me put a credits page into *FHMC Q*bert*. Not that many people saw it during its short-lived lifespan.

MARKETING Q*BERT

Even before the great coin returns and glowing articles in the press, upper management felt they might have a hit on their hands and prepared a marketing campaign to feature the hapless *Q*bert* in as many products and tie-ins as they could arrange. I had absolutely no involvement in any of this, but I have to give the marketing department credit, since they left no stone unturned. By the middle of 1983, *Q*bert* was everywhere! Lunchboxes, board games, card games, breakfast cereal, T-shirts, plush toys, figurines, wind-up toys, Frisbees, and more.

I can't remember getting anything for free, maybe a T-shirt which has long since disintegrated, but I felt compelled to buy the occasional piece of *Q*bert* merchandise when I came across one. Sadly, most of that stuff has disappeared over the years. All I have now is a *Q*bert* plush toy that my first-born son slept with when he was a baby.

The little noser was adored internally at Gottlieb as well. Chris Brewer, a programmer who was also a rather talented artist, drew up a 1983 *Q*bert* monthly calendar that popped up on a lot of cubicle walls within the company. He also created something called the *Q*bert* Qoloring Book, which had pages and pages of Q-related puns with accompanying pictures. Some examples: Q*lius Caesar, Q*beard the Pirate, and JaQ*e Q*steau.

In 1982, Coca-Cola purchased Columbia Pictures and thus became our parent company. While I was working on *FHMC Q*bert*, word came down from management that Coca-Cola wanted us to create a unique version of original *Q*bert* to

Excerpt from the *Q*bert* Qalendar. (Artwork by Chris Brewer.)

promote their Mello Yello soft drink. Luckily we didn't have to make too many changes. Jeff supplied their logo

Excerpt from the *Q*bert* Qoloring Book. (Artwork by Chris Brewer.)

art, which I added to the title screen. We also added a new screen that appeared every couple of rounds, showing our orange hero flying on a disk and circling a large can of Mello Yello before affixing his nose to a straw and sucking it down. I remember suggesting we lose the straw and have Q*bert's nose getting longer until it became the straw, but either Gottlieb's management or Coca-Cola nixed that idea.

I also have some vague memories of a 7-Eleven tie-in, which replaced the Mello Yello logo with 7-Eleven's and the soda can with a Slurpee cup, but I don't remember if that was ever released. I re-used it in *FHMC Q*bert*, but with a generic cup. After each bonus screen, there's a tally screen to add up your bonus points where *Q*bert* flies around a Slurpee-like drink and guess what? His nose extends to become the straw!

As an interesting side note, once the Coca-Cola deal to purchase Columbia Pictures was finalized, all of the Pepsi machines at Gottlieb were replaced with Coke machines. I suppose it made business sense, but it pissed the hell out of the Pepsi drinkers. I had no favorite soft drink myself, so there was no outrage from me, but there sure was a lot of water cooler talk about it.

CHAPTER FIVE

THE AFTERMATH

With the success of Q*bert, it was inevitable that home versions would be produced. I was pretty much uninvolved in that process, but I did write up some descriptions of the internal logic of the game (enemy release tables and round progressions) to send to the home version developers. I even had a few phone calls with some of them when they had questions. The first time I saw any of the home versions was at the Consumer Electronics Show in Chicago, where they were introduced. Home game systems at that time were pretty crude compared to what was in the arcades, and I remember being horrified by some versions (Atari 2600—yipes!) and pretty impressed with others (like ColecoVision).

Also inevitable was management's desire for a sequel. In all honesty, I hadn't thought about one. I was pretty adamant that *FHMC Q*bert* was a re-tuning rather than a sequel, and I'd been too busy working on it and the original game before that to think about what to do next at all. It was astounding to me that I'd gotten to do one video game on my own, and I was still basking in that accomplishment slightly when they asked me about a sequel.

I remember Howie and Ron tried to pitch me on the *Q*lympics*, a *Q*bert*-themed *Track & Field* kind of game. I wasn't against it—I just didn't want to do it. Sam Russo started to develop it, and it went through some conceptual design, but for some reason it never went anywhere. The more I thought about it, the less interested I was in doing *any* other *Q*bert*-related game. For one thing, I felt the color-changing cube-hopping premise was played out, and to me that's what made the game unique. Take that away, and you're just throwing Q*bert into different situations where he could be any character, really. After *FHMC Q*bert*, I couldn't see what I could add that would be interesting enough to want to spend more time on him. Plus, I felt there was a whole universe of new ideas that I hadn't explored yet, and I wanted to try my hand at one of those. Making another *Q*bert* game seemed like a step backwards.

Do I have any regrets about that decision? Maybe some. But honestly, it was the right decision for me at the time. Years later, when interest in classic arcade games resurfaced, I did think of some ideas for a new *Q*bert* game, but have yet to be given an opportunity to explore them.

After I'd made it definitively clear that I didn't want to work on a sequel, fellow programmer Neil Burnstein approached me. Neil was newly hired, looking for a game to do, and had an idea for a *Q*bert* game. He kindly asked if I would be okay with him pursuing it, and I gave him my blessing. He went and made *Q*bert's Qubes*.

The wrinkle that made *Q*bert's Qubes* different was that, rather than a pyramid of cubes, Q*bert hops from one floating cube to another. The colors on the cubes don't change, but when Q*bert hops off a cube, it rotates in the direction of his hop, changing the orientation of the cube faces. Three faces of each cube are visible at any given time. In order to complete the round you need to rotate each cube so that its visible colors are in the same orientation as the target cube. There are some variations on that theme as you progress, but that's the basic gist.

Personally, I felt it was a bit complicated and maybe lacked some of the whimsy of the original, but it was Neil's baby and I let him run with it.

*Q*bert* also got his own pinball game: *Q*bert's Quest,* courtesy of legendary pinball designer and Gottlieb employee John Trudeau. That was kind of a thrill, as I was a huge pinball fan.

My little noser was becoming quite the celebrity. But once I was done with *FHMC Q*bert*, we said "bye-bye" to each other, and I tried to figure out what to do next.

While I was in the thick of making *Q*bert*, I didn't think much about what else was going on in the industry. I had a pretty singular focus on completing the game, and that lasted until the *Q*bert* cabinets were rolling off the production line. Even then, I became a little obsessed with correcting what I perceived to be my mistakes by immersing myself in *FHMC Q*bert*.

But after that, I had more time to pay attention to what was going on around me. And there was lots of activity, both internally and in the rest of the industry. Checking out the competition was something of a necessity. It was very common for us to bring competitors' games in-house and play the crap out of them. It helped to inspire us or let us know we should be worried about falling behind.

The year 1983 introduced a sensation to the video arcade world that would find Gottlieb (and a lot of other manufacturers) playing catch-up. It was called *Dragon's Lair.* Made by Cinematronics, *Dragon's Lair* was basically an interactive animated movie. The animation was of the highest quality, created by former Disney animator Don Bluth. Full-screen, movie-quality graphics in a video game! It was unheard of!

The technological miracle that made this possible

was the LaserDisc. A LaserDisc was basically a storage device for movie playback with resolution superior to the recently introduced VHS and Beta videotapes. It looked like a DVD (which of course didn't exist back then), but was about a foot in diameter. The first consumer LaserDisc players became available in 1978, but Cinematronics was the first company to exploit its use for video games and everybody went bonkers.

Dragon's Lair essentially just played back its animation on the arcade game's monitor but more importantly, it also allowed players to interact with it at key times. The technology that made this possible was a special model of LaserDisc player manufactured by Pioneer. It had an interface that allowed an external device (like a computer or video game hardware) to control the LaserDisc. Functions like Stop, Start, Seek, and Play could be controlled by game software, which resulted in LaserDiscs gaining an essential video game quality: interactivity.

Gottlieb absolutely needed to jump on this bandwagon. Not only was the graphical improvement over current games astonishing, but Gottlieb also knew that every other manufacturer would begin working on it (if they weren't already). A new hardware engineer, Dave Pfeiffer, was hired to design an interface between our game hardware and the Pioneer LaserDisc player. Conceptually the change was simple—we would replace our background plane with the output of the LaserDisc. Our foreground plane of sprites would stay the same.

Once Dave designed and implemented his interface, programmers Chris Brewer and Fred Darmstadt wrote the software to control it. Together, they made Gottlieb's first LaserDisc game, *M.A.C.H. 3*, referring to both the speed of sound and an acronym they'd made up: "Military Air Command Hunter." It was a fighter jet game that used actual aerial movie footage overlaid with our

Creating Q*bert

standard sprite-based foreground. I'll have more to say about *M.A.C.H. 3* in the next chapter. For now, just know it was released to great success in the latter half of 1983, earning the number-one "Player's Choice" title in *Replay Magazine*.

WHAT'S IN A NAME?

A significant change occurred in 1983 that resulted in *M.A.C.H. 3* going out the door without the Gottlieb name on it. For some reason unknown to me and most of my fellow employees, upper management decided to give the company a new name with a new logo. I'm pretty sure this had something to do with Coca-Cola's purchase of Columbia Pictures, but I couldn't be certain. Perhaps it was an attempt to distance the video division from Gottlieb's pinball roots, which was perceived as a dying industry. I don't know.

Even though the company was no longer owned by the Gottlieb family, Alvin Gottlieb, son of founder David, would still stop by for an occasional visit just to see what was going on. Alvin clearly had a fondness for pinball and his father's legacy and was beloved by the pinball division, most of whom had been working there since the days when the company was family-run. So the idea of changing the company's name didn't sit well with many of us who were proud of its history, especially the old-timers.

But the decision was made, and a company-wide meeting was announced. I remember it well.

The president of the company, Boyd Browne (a man who was rarely seen down "in the trenches") stood before the collected group of employees from every department, in front of a large covered piece of cardboard on an easel. He ceremoniously removed the cover and unveiled a large letter "M" with a star nestled on top of it, and the name MYLSTAR. I knew they'd hired a marketing firm to brainstorm and research for months before coming up with this. Seeing the new name for the first time, I remember thinking, "I hope management didn't pay them a lot of money." Because my next thought, which I voiced aloud instantly, was, "Has anyone noticed that that's 'Rat Slym' spelled backwards?"

I don't know what possessed me to say it out loud. I wasn't generally a smart-ass, although, having grown up in Brooklyn, that particular trait is never far from my reach. I guess I thought it might get a laugh. And it did. An uproarious laugh from pretty much everyone as they all realized it was true. Everyone except Boyd Browne, who looked absolutely horrified and furious at the same time.

Seems to me, if you pay a company to create a new name for you, they should at least consider what it says when you spell it backwards. But there it was. We were now Mylstar. All of our video games, beginning with *M.A.C.H. 3*, would be released under the Mylstar name. New pinball games also had the Mylstar logo, but in a concession to the company's history, they also carried the label "A Gottlieb pinball

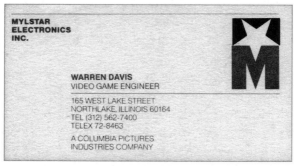

Yet another business card, but this time with the cool and very expensive Mylstar name and logo.

Creating Q*bert

game." To me personally, the company remained Gottlieb and I'll continue to refer to it that way here (although a reference to Mylstar may slip in every once in a while, possibly ironically).

DOWNTIME

After *FHMC Q*bert* was officially shelved, I found myself with a lot of downtime. Some *Q*bert*-related work was yet to come (mostly conversations with developers of the home versions), but I was basically without a project.

There's a feeling I always get at the end of any major endeavor. It's a sort of restlessness. Maybe you've felt this too at some point. You get so used to having an endless list of to-do items on your plate, especially as a project races to its conclusion. Then it ends and your plate is empty, and it just feels . . . well, weird. Wrong. Uncomfortable. But sooner or later, you realize it's okay to exhale and maybe relax a bit. So I took the opportunity to clean up my desk, which, after any months-long project, tends to resemble a garbage dump of papers (most likely with some actual garbage in there as well).

Taking a breather also meant looking around and noticing changes, and there were a quite a few. Howie and Ron had been staffing up with new programmers, so there were some new faces around. And there were lots more games in development.

Kan Yabumoto, whose use of the Escher cube pattern inspired me to create the *Q*bert* pyramid, had been working on a space shooter called *Mad Planets*. Featuring art by Jeff Lee and sounds by Dave Thiel, it became the next Gottlieb video game after *Q*bert* to go into production, and was very well-received.

Sam Russo was busy making a Three Stooges game

The Aftermath

that was in development for an unusually long year and a half before its eventual release.

Fred Darmstadt and Chris Brewer were in the early stages of developing the aforementioned LaserDisc game *M.A.C.H. 3*.

Tim Skelly was contracted to do a second game for Gottlieb, and was off somewhere creating it. He'd pop in every once in a while to show us his progress.

Recent hires Chris Kreubel and Matt Householder were developing a game based on the upcoming Columbia feature film *Krull*. The game turned out pretty well, but the movie, to Columbia's dismay, tanked.

And then there was the aforementioned Neil Burnstein, who was sinking his teeth into *Q*bert*'s *Qubes*.

In the coming months, more coders were hired: Jon Coyle, Joe Ulewicz, Steve Pacheco, and Lyn Oswald.

And I found myself, with all things *Q*bert* behind me, in much the same situation as when I'd finished my work on *Pro-Vid-Guard-Argus*. I was expected to make a game! But the difference this time was that I was no longer a neophyte with no games under my belt. Now I was someone who'd proven himself by not just finishing a game, but delivering a successful one. Howie and Ron thought (wisely, I might add), "Hey, if this guy could produce a successful game the first time out of the gate, maybe we should just leave him alone and see what he comes up with next." And they did.

Ideas had popped into my head over the previous few months that seemed worth exploring. Some were graphical ideas—ways to bring a third dimension into gameplay, sometimes more so than *Q*bert* did—and some were ideas for new gameplay mechanics. Now I had the time to explore them.

I stuck with the process I had used for *Q*bert*, starting with an idea and fleshing it out as I went along. I never really had an end game in sight, and with some of these concepts, it showed. I developed them to a point, and then either became unclear on where to go next or got bored with them. My "standards" were high now—too high, maybe. I became infatuated with the notion of doing something different. Something unique. I wasn't interested in just rehashing a game or style of gameplay that already existed.

THE FLY GAME

One exploration that proved fruitful began with a question: "Since joysticks are controlled by human hands, what if you used them to manipulate onscreen images of actual human hands?"

This would require larger images on the screen than we'd ever used with our hardware. Our system used foreground sprites that were only 16 pixels square. Coily was actually two sprites, one atop the other, moving as one. It wouldn't take much to apply the same principle to attach as many as six sprites together to create a nice-size hand.

But what would you do with those hands? Well, at the time I found myself killing a lot of houseflies. They were ever-present in both my house and my mind, as was the desire to kill as many of them as possible. How cool would it be to control a hand with a joystick, move it toward an airborne fly, then press a button on the end of the joystick to close your hand into a fist, thus squishing said fly. That sounded kinda fun to me. Gross, maybe, but fun, and certainly less gross than squishing a real fly.

I thought back to one of the original video arcade games, *Spacewar!* It was a two-player game, with one player shooting things on the left side of the screen, and the other shooting things on the right. You each got a point for everything you destroyed. A simple player-versus-player model was just what I needed. I asked Jeff Lee to create the art and, as usual, he did not disappoint. I got a floating, open hand image that was as realistic as possible (given the limited number of colors available) and detached at the wrist in a clean, non-gruesome way, along with an animation that closed it into a fist. Jeff also supplied a fly animation along with a static image of a crushed fly.

Coding up the game wasn't very difficult. There was no background behind the two player hands, just a solid color—sky blue. The foreground was filled with flies moving randomly around the screen. The control panel consisted of two joysticks, each controlling a different hand. Pressing the thumb buttons atop each stick made your virtual hand close into a fist.

Becoming skilled at this game took a little bit of practice. You had to position your "hand" so that a fly was right in the middle of your open palm, then press the button to squish it. If you succeeded, a dead fly would plummet down off-screen when your hand opened, much like Q*bert falling into the abyss. The flies moved about randomly, which made it challenging, but I played around with the hit detection so it wouldn't seem unfair. Each game was timed. Whoever squished more flies after three minutes of play was the winner.

The craziest thing about this game was the way people at the office took to it. They loved it! There was a bit of a repulsive attraction to it, since Jeff's flies and hands actually looked somewhat real. So when you played it, your brain went to a place where you sorta felt like you were actually killing flies.

We set the game up in a cabinet outside my cubicle. People would come over and play it when they were on a break or passing by, or maybe just to take their mind off work for a few minutes. And it got played a lot! There was just something gratifying about it, and it was kind of addictive. The cabinet stayed out there for weeks, if not months. At the time, it was a fun diversion and nothing more. But the concept would return later on.

*Q*BERT* GOES MAINSTREAM

As 1983 progressed, it seemed there was no stopping the *Q*bert* juggernaut. The April issue of *Vidiot* magazine had a full-page photo of John Cougar (later to be known as John Mellencamp) leaning on a *Q*bert* cabinet and smiling. Mentions of the game started to appear not just in video game magazines, but in mainstream

In 1983, it seemed *Q*bert* was being talked about everywhere—not just video game magazines with celebrity photos, but in mainstream publications like *The New Yorker, USA Today,* and *Glamour* (!!)

publications as well. In the comics section of your local paper, an ad for Hi-C's *Q*bert* Sweepstakes promised two full-size *Q*bert* arcade games as grand prizes. The August 29 issue of the *New Yorker* has a *Q*bert* anecdote in its "Talk of the Town" column. There was also a blurb about the game in the August 1983 issue of *Glamour* magazine. *Glamour*! Can you believe that? Its popularity was only aided by the release of all the home cartridge versions that year.

The most surreal event I experienced, though, was seeing the little noser in a Saturday morning cartoon series. Perhaps some of you reading this might remember the *Saturday Supercade* cartoon, which debuted in the fall of 1983 and lasted two seasons. It featured characters from *Q*bert, Frogger, Donkey Kong, Donkey Kong Jr., Pitfall!, Space Ace,* and *Kangaroo* in their own short individual cartoons.

I don't really have much to say about the choices made in adapting *Q*bert* to the non-interactive small screen. The cartoon version of Q*bert had arms and wore sneakers and a letterman jacket. He attended Q-Burg High School with his girlfriend Q*tee, his brother Q*bit, and his friends Q*val, Q*ball, and Q*mongus. I'm cringing as I write this. As you may have surmised, neither I nor anyone else at Gottlieb had anything to do with this cartoon series. I remember most of us thinking it was kind of ridiculous. If we'd been given an opportunity to pitch our own *Q*bert* cartoon, it would have been very different, and possibly un-airable by network standards.

Then, the following year, Q*bert hopped from the small screen to the big screen. In the movie *Moscow on the Hudson*, there's a scene in which Robin Williams's character is playing a *Q*bert* arcade game and makes the little guy jump off the pyramid. There's an extreme close-up of the screen as that happens. My game, bigger than life in a Robin Williams movie! Now that was a surreal moment for me.

It shouldn't have surprised me too much, though. *Moscow on the Hudson* was a Columbia Picture, and Columbia owned the rights to *Q*bert*, so they didn't have to pay anyone for its use in the film. In an unconnected piece of trivia, I'd heard a rumor once that Robin Williams was a fan of Q*bert's voice, and would mimic Q*bert's sounds on occasion. For years, I wondered if that were true. Many years later, I found myself standing near him after an event at a Los Angeles improv club. Sadly, I never found out the answer to my question; I couldn't get up the nerve to approach him and ask.

As enormously satisfying as it was for me to watch Q*bert-mania spread across the land, the joy was eclipsed by a growing self-imposed pressure to come up with another idea for a game. And what's the best way to respond to building pressure? Toga party! Well, actually no. For me, it was: get married! In the spring, my girlfriend of two years and I flew to California. We spent a few days seeing the sights there and then took a road trip with some friends to Las Vegas, where we met up with close family members and got hitched. It wasn't a spur-of-the-moment elopement; we actually planned it ahead of time. Just a very small ceremony, with the buffet at the MGM Grand as our reception. The trip doubled as our honeymoon. Then it was back to California, back to Chicago, and back to work.

BUNNY BONDAGE

This idea got pretty far.

One of the aspects of video games that has always intrigued me is the ability to simulate real-world physics.

For example, even though it was kind of a small and simple thing, I really enjoyed implementing gravity on Q*bert, and I mentioned earlier how adding the slight bounce in his knees when he lands on a cube was also very satisfying. In looking for new things to explore, I thought of objects in motion colliding and the way their paths change as a result. This was certainly nothing new in the world of video games. *Pong* was designed around the principle of a ball bouncing off walls and floating paddles controlled by players. But during my post-Q*bert downtime, I hadn't seen that mechanic used in a game with a player character.

I envisioned a player character who carried a shield. Since I lived in a world of 8-way joysticks, I pictured the shield as an octagon with three of the eight sides missing. The five existing sides would be centered in front of the player, leaving him vulnerable from behind. The advantage of having the shields made of straight lines was that it simplified the math of computing collision paths. A curved shield would require more trigonometry, and we didn't really have the computing power to do that.

The mechanics of this idea involved hurtling objects toward the player from different directions. The player would have to turn and block each attack with the shield to make an object ricochet away. If something hit from behind, the player, having no shield there, would die. Whereas in most games, you run away from the dangerous objects, in this scenario, you'd be safest running *into* them.

Here's where it gets a little weird. When I was a kid, there was a cartoon character on TV called Ricochet Rabbit. For some reason, that name got stuck in my head when I first thought of this concept, and from then on I could only imagine that the objects flying at the player should be rabbits. Never one to shy away from the surreal,

I asked Jeff to create the art I needed, and in true Jeff fashion, he delivered exactly that. Next thing you knew, bunny rabbits were flying around my screen. A player character with a five-sided shield could deflect them back the way they came, or ricochet them at a 45-degree angle, depending on which part of the shield they hit.

I never actually tried to rationalize why killer bunnies would be flying through the air, but I did need to give the game a goal. So I kept most of the screen open, but lined the top and bottom with open cages connected to an outer rim wall. If you could get a bunny to fly into an open cage, the door closed and it was contained, no longer a threat. Otherwise, the bunny would bounce off the door and continue flying across the screen. The playfield looked like some kind of arena, so I added a Monty Python-esque introduction of the player entering from off-screen—held by a hand with a telescoping arm—and being dropped down into the center of the arena.

I knew we would never actually be able to use the name Ricochet Rabbit, as it was already a trademarked property, but the nature of the game offered another bit of alliteration. It became known as *Bunny Bondage*, or *Bunnies in Bondage*. It looked good and it was fun, but it wasn't quite enough to satisfy me. The game already had the pseudo-3D look of *Q*bert*, so I started experimenting with adding a pseudo-3D maze, something I had never seen. The visual challenge here was that parts of the maze might obscure the player if he appeared to be "behind" a wall. Since the maze was made up of background blocks and the player was a foreground object, this required a bit of programming trickery to sell the illusion.

The maze was both fun and satisfying to accomplish. What was becoming unsatisfying was figuring out how to turn this strange game into a releasable product.

I worked on *Bunny Bondage* for what felt like an

eternity, but it was probably just a couple of months. It seemed to have a lot going for it—it looked different, it had the same kind of quirky whimsical tone as *Q*bert*, and people around the office seemed to enjoy playing it. Management was excited about it and wanted to know when they could put it on the schedule. But I kept putting them off, saying it wasn't ready. The reality was that as much as I enjoyed the concept and the look and how it played, I didn't know how to complete it. I played around with it a lot, added things, changed things. After a while it felt like I was just spinning my wheels.

And then one day I was approached by Dennis Nordman, a recent hire who was unique at Gottlieb in that he was neither a programmer nor an artist. He was a concept guy, and he had a concept he wanted to run by me. Today, Dennis is known as a legendary pinball designer, having created such classics as *Elvira and the Party Monsters*, *White Water*, and *Demolition Man*, among many others. But that all came later. When he approached me in late summer of 1983, he was just a guy looking for a programmer to collaborate with on a concept he was developing. It was a LaserDisc game, intended to be sold as a kit for *M.A.C.H. 3* cabinets. You may remember from the previous chapter that a "kit" was a low-cost means of converting one game (presumably no longer earning much money) into a newer, more desirable game.

The success of *M.A.C.H. 3*, as well as a growing number of our competitors' LaserDisc games, convinced management that this technology was a genuine phenomenon and possibly a permanent game changer in the video arcade industry. Gottlieb needed more LaserDisc games in development, but was also aware that LaserDisc games were more expensive than non-LaserDisc games. For one thing, you had to generate the video content, which wasn't cheap. Also, *M.A.C.H. 3* had a cockpit-style cabinet option that allowed the player to sit as if they were really piloting a jet. These models were particularly pricey, and when *M.A.C.H. 3*'s popularity started to wane (which it undoubtedly would at some point), operators would want another game they could swap into those same cabinets without having to buy all new hardware. So whatever LaserDisc game came next after *M.A.C.H. 3*, management wanted the ability to sell it as a kit.

The ideal game for a *M.A.C.H. 3* kit would use the same control panel and monitor orientation as *M.A.C.H. 3*, so the kit would just contain a new marquee, new cabinet and control panel artwork, new ROMs, and a different LaserDisc. By installing these into their original *M.A.C.H. 3* cabinet, operators would have a new game for a fraction of the price.

It didn't take long for Dennis to talk me into jumping on board. I was very jazzed about working on a LaserDisc game, and I loved his concept. Plus, this was just the excuse I needed to put aside *Bunny Bondage*. I told myself I would come back to it after this new project was finished, but I never did. Looking back, I really wish I had. The mechanic of using the shield as both a defense and a means of re-directing flying objects at your enemies was really unique and fun. I just couldn't see how to put it all together at the time.

A BITTERSWEET GOODBYE

One final change that 1983 brought to Gottlieb, just as I was getting involved with Dennis's sci-fi LaserDisc game, was the departure of Howie Rubin. This, in many ways, signaled the end of an era. Howie and Ron had built the video division from scratch, and Howie's influence in creating the work environment that led to the success of *Q*bert* and *M.A.C.H. 3* cannot be overstated. Howie believed the success of the video division should afford him some autonomy in moving the company forward, but he still had to justify all of his decisions to his bosses in upper management and didn't care much for that. He himself admits that perhaps his ego played a part in his dissatisfaction. Plus, he didn't like the direction the company was going, largely due to what seemed to be a more hands-on involvement from the corporate overlords at Columbia Pictures and their new owner, Coca-Cola. The switch from Gottlieb to Mylstar didn't sit well with him, either.

Perhaps the straw that broke the proverbial camel's back was when Columbia put pressure on Howie to eliminate the pinball division completely. He wasn't comfortable being the guy to lay off an entire department, especially not the department that the company had been founded upon. With Howie gone, that particular battle would have to be fought by others. And thankfully, it was won in the end. Pinball was scaled down while more resources were put into video games, but the department was never disbanded.

And so, Howie left for greener pastures, with a pay raise and part ownership of the company he was about to join. A bittersweet departure to be sure, with ramifications that took some time to fully manifest.

BONUSES AND ROYALTIES

Most people who meet me think I had some financial stake in *Q*bert*. Unfortunately, that's just not the case. Everyone hired at Gottlieb signed a form stating that anything developed while an employee was entirely owned by the company. So Gottlieb owned the rights to *Q*bert*, and the only thing Jeff, Dave, and I owned were bragging rights.

That's not to say the company didn't show their appreciation. One night, Ron Waxman called me into his office, then complimented me in the kindest of terms and expressed his gratitude for what I did for the company by handing me a bonus check for $20,000. That was a huge chunk of money for me, and I was extremely grateful. The timing was good, too. My wife was pregnant at the time with our first child, and we were living in an apartment with a roommate. That bonus check became the down payment on a condo in Chicago, the first piece of property we owned.

Months later, Gottlieb introduced a royalty program for game creators. It came on the heels of Chris Brewer and Fred Darmstadt's success with *M.A.C.H. 3*. We'd heard that other companies, like Williams and Stern, had royalty programs that typically gave a financial reward based on how many units of the game were sold after passing a certain number, not unlike some book publishers. Finally Gottlieb was going to join the club, so to speak, and we were all pretty excited to hear about it. Ron Waxman called a department meeting to let everyone know the details of this new program. I don't remember exactly how many units needed to be sold before royalties kicked in, but the piece of information that stuck in my gut when I heard it was that the program wasn't retroactive. It would only apply to new games, so *Q*bert* and the more recent *M.A.C.H. 3* were ineligible. On top of that, he used *Q*bert* as an example. He said, "If *Q*bert* had been made under the royalty program, Warren would have gotten a royalty in the neighborhood of $100,000."

My jaw dropped. As much as I appreciated the $20,000 bonus, this news stung. I tried not to let it sting for too long, but it did sting. I've said that money wasn't my motivation for the work I was doing, and that's absolutely true. As long as I had enough to pay my bills and enjoy life, I was happy. But damn—the thought of missing out on that $100,000 hurt like a splinter. In hindsight, I was a little naive about money, but still I have no regrets. And I'm pretty certain that up until the day Gottlieb folded, no one ever collected a penny under their royalty program.

I mentioned using my *Q*bert* bonus as a down payment on a condo in Chicago. When that happened, I felt like I was becoming a grown-up. (My job, thankfully, kept me from going too far down that road.) My condo was in a six-flat building on the outskirts of Chicago's Lincoln Park neighborhood. I remember the day I met our next-door neighbors. They were a very nice couple, not really much older than my wife and me. As we talked, the husband started to go off on a tangent about how upset he was because he'd just heard that the nearby 7-Eleven was going to bring in some video games.

"Really?" I asked. "Why does that bother you?"

"Well, you know, it brings in the wrong kind of people. Hanging out all the time. Playing these games. It's terrible."

"I see," I said.

Then he asked, "What do you do for a living?"

So I told him, "I make video games."

The look on his face was priceless, and then he started backpedaling. But I think I was able to give him a perspective that maybe he hadn't considered, and by the end of the conversation he seemed to be okay with at least waiting to see if the neighborhood would fall apart by having a couple of video games at the 7-Eleven.

Spoiler alert: it didn't.

I got another small bonus some months later,

although not of the financial kind. *Electronic Games Magazine* gave out awards every year and in 1984, *Q*bert* won for Most Innovative Coin-Op Game. Although the award technically went to Gottlieb (or rather, Mylstar), Ron gave it to me. I also got to take one of the *Q*bert* engineering samples home. I had to pay a small amount for it (I think it was a hundred dollars), but as far as I was concerned both then and now, it was definitely worth it. When I brought it home, I replaced the ROMs with my personal favorite version, *FHMC Q*bert*, and, with rare exceptions, they've remained in there to this day.

CHAPTER SIX

US VS. THEM

M.A.C.H. *3*'s **gameplay was** fairly straightforward. At the start of a game you were offered two modes. One was a bombing run, in which your view was above your fighter jet looking directly down at the ground. Targets on the ground were indicated by computer-generated overlays, and as you flew, you had to properly time your bomb drops to hit the marked targets while avoiding enemy fire. The other mode was from a view directly behind your fighter jet, looking forward, commonly known as a "third person" view. In this mode, your goal was to shoot down enemy aircraft and hit targets on the ground while, again, avoiding enemy fire. In both modes, the movie footage playing from the LaserDisc determined the speed and overall course of your plane, but you could maneuver within the confines of the screen.

The game was fun and challenging, with graphics that were a giant leap beyond what earlier video games offered, but there was no "story" to speak of. And that lack of story didn't seem to matter. The game was a big success for Gottlieb . . . or, should I say, Mylstar. And that success meant there were a lot of *M.A.C.H.* *3* cabinets out there, both upright and cockpit. As always, once earnings started to drop, those cabinets would be much more attractive to their owners if there was a replacement game that could go into them. Dennis Nordman had an idea for just such a game. He developed it with Rich Tracy, Gottlieb's art director, and Dave Faust, whose role at the company I can't for the life of me remember. They'd even come up with the title: *Us vs. Them.*

Since *Us vs. Them* was intended to be a replacement kit for *M.A.C.H. 3*, it needed to use the same control panel and monitor. And since *M.A.C.H. 3*'s control stick was designed for flight, Dennis, Rich, and Dave knew their new concept would also be a flying game. But they didn't want players to feel like they were just playing a different kind of *M.A.C.H. 3*. It had to be a fresh, exciting new experience.

To provide that, Dennis, Rich, and Dave decided that *Us vs. Them* would tell a story. They came up with an alien invasion story in which America's best fighter pilots would battle a swarm of extraterrestrial enemies in the skies all across the U.S. This being a LaserDisc game, the plan was to once again use aerial footage as a backdrop, although, unlike *M.A.C.H. 3*, there wouldn't be any ground targets. The flying footage would simply provide background visuals and the illusion of very fast motion, while a programmer would have to supply whatever computer-generated gameplay was needed in the foreground.

So when Dennis came to me late in the summer of 1983 and asked if I'd be interested in programming a new LaserDisc game with a B-movie science-fiction theme, I immediately said yes. I'd been a sci-fi fan all my life. I grew up on a steady diet of sci-fi B-movies on TV, and most of the books I read were science fiction. This was right up my alley. When I asked what the gameplay should be, Dennis's answer was simple: he didn't have a clue. That would be my department.

The sci-fi/alien invasion theme already distinguished *Us vs. Them* from *M.A.C.H. 3*, but another idea of theirs really stepped things up a notch. They wanted to shoot background footage all over the country at familiar, iconic locations. They put together a wish list of places to include as backdrops, including the Statue of Liberty and Mount Rushmore. They had no idea how they were going to get footage of any of these places. Maybe stock footage? It was just a pipe dream at that point.

Dennis had another thought for setting this game apart from *M.A.C.H. 3*. He didn't just want the story explained in the attract mode. He wanted it to progress throughout the game—with a plot, just like in a movie, with a script and actors and sets. Even without knowing what our budget would be, we knew we couldn't reach Hollywood levels of filmmaking. But this was supposed to emulate a cheesy B-movie, and we were pretty sure we could achieve that.

I loved the idea, but I was a little skeptical that telling a full story would work in an arcade game. After all, we needed the game to collect quarters, and watching a movie is not an interactive experience. I didn't think people would enjoy watching parts of a movie while they played a video game. Silly me. Full motion-video cut scenes would become a standard of many home video games about ten years later. And *Dragon's Lair* was essentially just watching a cartoon, except every now and then you had to push your joystick in a particular direction to avoid dying. You might conclude that I wasn't a big fan of *Dragon's Lair*, and you'd be right. I appreciated the graphical breakthrough that it was, but I didn't think it was interactive enough. If you memorized the pattern and timing of joystick pushes, getting through it became very mechanical.

I thought about how to integrate a story into the game, and eventually concluded that if we kept the snippets of storytelling short enough—ten to fifteen seconds at most, followed by a minute of traditional interactive

Creating Q*bert

gameplay—maybe that would work. The story scenes could act as short breathers between levels of intense action. While *Dragon's Lair* (and later *Space Ace*, which had not yet been released) was just a slightly interactive animated movie, and *M.A.C.H. 3* was a standard video game with filmed backgrounds, this would be a hybrid of both styles using live actors. It had never been done before, and I started to get really excited.

During one of our brainstorming sessions, another suggestion popped up about how to make the game more movie-like. What if the game changed camera angles during gameplay? After all, a war movie never stays at just one camera angle during a dogfight. It cuts from one view to another. While it sounded like a good idea, I just didn't see how it could work. If you're looking in one direction and you shoot at something, and then the game cuts to another angle, not only is it jarring and disorienting, but you might not be able to tell if you actually hit your target. And with enemies shooting at you, a change in angle could increase your chance of not seeing something that's about to hit you.

The rest of the team mulled it over and agreed, with some disappointment. Still, I kept thinking about it and, after some pondering, came up with a possible compromise. Rather than change angles within the same level, we could have the viewpoint change from one level to another. So, for example, you might be flying one mission from a viewpoint behind your fighter jet, looking forward, then after a bonus recap and a short story scene, the next mission might play like a horizontal side scroller. Of course, this would be a burden to programming since every point of view would have to be implemented with unique code. It would almost be like coding different games. It also made the requirements of our flying footage much more specific. But the idea seemed so cool and unique that everyone jumped on board wholeheartedly.

Another thing that seemed like a perfect fit for *Us vs. Them* was a new feature showing up in some arcade games at the time: the "continue" option. This would allow a player to add a quarter or two after their game ended and continue playing from where they left off. We decided to implement it, but first we needed to figure out how long the entire game would be, which was partly determined by how much movie footage we could fit on a LaserDisc.

As if we weren't setting our sights high enough, I had yet another idea that would further complicate our efforts. I decided it would be really cool if each level had a number of alternate background choices (randomly selected) so that every time you played the game, you'd have a different visual experience. I loved the idea of flying over different places each time you played—but that would require a lot more flying footage. And due to Laser-Disc storage limitations, every alternate scene we added to the disc reduced the total number of levels in the game.

In the end we had to make some compromises, but we were able to fit one or two alternates into a few of the levels. When you started a new game, you might've been flying through clouds, cruising over San Francisco Bay, or soaring over Lake Powell. In the final design, *Us vs. Them* from start to finish had around twenty minutes of gameplay with thirteen levels.

SHIFTING VIEWS AND CHANGING BUTTONS

With all of us excited about the potential of our concept, Dennis, Rich, and Dave went off to come up with a story and a script, while I started writing the program. I had a little bit of learning to do as far as controlling the Laser-Disc player. Our LaserDisc hardware worked by replacing what used to be the background plane with movie footage, but our foreground was essentially the same sprite-based system as *Reactor* or *Q*bert*. The flight stick had a trigger and two thumb buttons for shooting. I decided that, unlike *M.A.C.H. 3*, the player would always shoot in bursts that came simultaneously from the tips of each wing. This gave a nice sense of depth as pairs of bullets appeared to converge and shrink in the distance. I also used the two control panel buttons differently from *M.A.C.H. 3*, varying their functions based on the camera angle of that level.

There are three basic camera angles in *Us vs. Them*. One is directly behind your fighter jet. Technically, this should be called a "first-third person" view, since you see the plane in front of you, but we called it "first-person" for simplicity. (Usually, "first-person" would mean seeing through the eyes of the player. In a true first-person flying game, your view would be of the cockpit.) During our first-person levels, the control panel buttons allow you to roll your plane right and left. Since your shots come from the tips of your wings, rolling your plane could be used strategically to control your aim. The second angle is a side view that essentially makes the game play like a horizontal scroller. We called this "profile," and in levels with this view, the buttons toggle between shooting forward or backward, since your plane can "speed up" to be at the right of the screen, or "slow down" to be on the left. The final viewpoint is above the jet, looking slightly down so that the horizon is just off the top of the screen. We named this "bird's-eye." Once again, the buttons change the direction of fire toward either the top of the screen (in front of you) or the bottom (behind). For one level, this viewpoint is reversed, so your fighter jet is in the distance flying toward you.

The different angles of view meant I was essentially programming different games, but the gameplay was simple enough that I wasn't too worried about it. The only real challenge was in the first-person perspective. As I've said before, our hardware wasn't fast enough to do lots of trigonometric calculations, which is what would normally be required to simulate a 3D perspective. Luckily, Chris Brewer and Fred Darmstadt had worked out a method for *M.A.C.H. 3* to give the illusion of depth with a minimum of computation. They passed that method on to me, and I used it on *Us vs. Them*, as well as a number of other games throughout my career.

Jeff Lee designed the fighter jet and did all of our overlaid graphics. He made a tiny cardboard model that could fit in your hand and used it as an eyeball reference as he hand-pixeled sprites of all the jet angles I would need. The jet was mostly gray, so I could allocate a few different shades to it and make it look as realistic as possible, which it did. Another testament to Jeff's remarkable abilities.

STORY AND SCRIPT

Having a concept of an alien invasion was one thing, but coming up with a detailed story and a script that we could actually film was quite another. Plus, we weren't telling the story in a conventional way, since each scene was intended to be just a few seconds long. We decided not to try breaking any new ground in the annals of science fiction. We just needed to come up with a typical story (clichés and all) and let it unfold in very small chunks. Once we settled on how many levels the game would have, we knew how many scenes we had to write.

Dennis took the first crack at it, and I thought what he came up with was pretty good. I did a pass on it, attempting to improve some dialogue or add tension. The scenes all took place in the control room, where our heroic commander was keeping tabs on his fighter pilots.

Speaking of fighter pilots, there were six different pilots to account for why the flying scenes would be taking place (we hoped) at locations all over the country. The pilots all had color-coded nicknames: Mean Green, Big

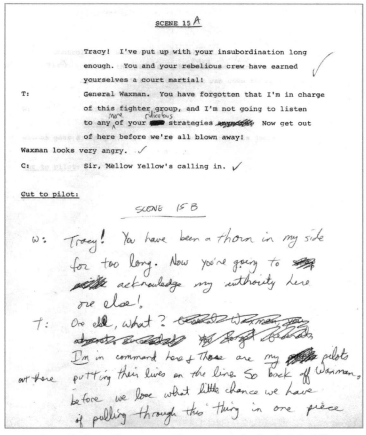

A page from the *Us vs. Them* script. There were multiple, slightly different versions of most scenes. This has my notes as well as an alternate to the original scene written by Dennis.

Red, Quicksilver, Mellow Yellow, White Knight, and Sky Blue. Their nicknames matched the color of their helmets—an attempt to easily distinguish between them.

The first few scenes of the script established the storytelling framework, the characters, and the battles. Then our antagonist shows up, a four-star general who seems to just want to give everybody grief. Later in the game—spoiler alert!—one pilot is believed lost, but actually he's entered the alien mothership and eventually saves the day by completing a special level at the end of the game. After that level, the final scene reveals the general to be an alien spy who escapes by transporting out of the control room ... The End? And then the president of the United States gives you a congratulatory speech and instructs you on how to enter your initials into the high score table.

With the basic conceptual and story work done, we now had to actually start generating some flying footage. The only problem was . . . we really had no idea how to do that. Since our desired viewpoints were very specific, it became clear that stock footage wouldn't work. We had to hire someone to shoot it all. To this day, I don't know what our budget was, but it had to have been substantial. Management, basking in the success of *Q*bert* and *M.A.C.H. 3*, must have been feeling pretty confident in themselves. With the coffers undoubtedly filled with some extra cash, they were willing to splurge.

So we moved forward, with one not-so-minor wrinkle: we were given a deadline. This was new. Under Howie's rule, we'd all worked at whatever pace was needed to explore and fine-tune our games. We hadn't had much pressure in the way of deadlines. That being said, new games were generally introduced at the two major trade shows of the coin-op industry, the AMOA in the fall, and the Amusement Operators Expo (AOE) in the spring. We were informed by Howie's replacement, Frank Ballouz, that management wanted to show this game at next February's AOE—less than six months away. We had no idea if that deadline was possible, but we wanted to believe it was, and we dedicated ourselves to making it happen.

FLYING FOOTAGE

Once we knew stock footage wasn't an option, we had to figure out how to get the flying footage we needed. That meant hiring someone more knowledgeable than us and communicating our very specific needs to them. Luckily, *M.A.C.H. 3* had paved our way by using Clay Lacy Jets, based in Burbank, California, to shoot their footage. I believe it was Rich Tracy who took on the role of internal producer at this point, hiring them once again for this new project, though I wasn't aware of any of this at the time. From my perspective, things just came together magically. Somehow we also hooked up with a small VFX company in Los Angeles to act as our off-site producers, to coordinate all the flying shoots and also create the few special effects shots we'd need of the alien mothership. They just needed some direction to get started, and soon, Dennis and I found ourselves on a plane to California.

It had been a few months since I'd flown to Los Angeles for my Vegas wedding. Before that, my only visit to L.A. had been in 1978 to visit John Craig, my best friend from college who at the time was working at NASA's Jet Propulsion Lab in Pasadena. Although I'd traveled a lot during my time at Bell Labs, this would be my first business trip working for Gottlieb, and I was kind of excited. Air travel back then was much different than it is now. Our plane was a 747 wide-body with a passenger lounge and bar on the upstairs level. This plane could hold upwards of three hundred passengers, but our

Me, wearing a Mylstar T-shirt, overlooking a smoggy San Fernando Valley, utterly oblivious to the motion sickness I will experience shortly.

flight had about fifteen people on it. I spent much of the flight walking around the nearly empty plane. When we arrived, we rented a car at the airport and drove to the Sheraton Universal.

Once we got settled, we found our producers, a couple of very nice fellows whose names escape me, but who were the coolest guys to us because they worked in the movie business. The first thing they did was show us a mock-up of what they were planning for our mothership levels, which occur later in the game after one of the fighter pilots enters the mothership. These levels were intended to act like bonus rounds. There's no shooting necessary and no enemy fire to avoid. Instead, you fly through the tunnels of the mothership, which have "energy walls" that zap your shield power if you touch them. Luckily, these walls all have at least one plane-size hole so you can get through safely if you position and orient your plane to match the hole. But as the game progresses, the holes get smaller and require some very specific maneuvering to avoid getting zapped.

For our game, our new L.A. friends had built a tunnel about twenty feet long with a weird light show happening around it. On top of that, they had composited a series of circular walls with shapes cut out to form the holes that the player's jet could pass through. Of course, what they showed us wasn't complete. It was basically a proof of concept, but still we were pretty impressed that anyone was putting any effort into this. We also gave them photos and drawings of the player-controlled fighter jet that Jeff had designed, so they could incorporate it into a few short cut scenes involving the mothership.

Next, we took a drive over to Burbank Airport, where the real fun would begin. We were going to shoot some flying footage! We arrived at the hangar of Clay Lacy Jets and found, waiting for us on the tarmac, a Learjet with a nose camera and belly camera, both of which could be operated from inside the plane. The interior of the plane contained lots of equipment and we must have had around eight people trying to fit inside, so it was kind of cramped. I'd flown in a Piper Cub once when I was a child, but never in a small jet. I found myself in a constant state of fascination. Everything about this trip

The hangar at Clay Lacy Jets with a Learjet fueled and ready for us.

was awesome! Well, almost everything, as I would soon find out.

Our plan was to fly to Arizona and shoot some footage of Lake Powell, then catch some other types of terrain on the return trip. We started off by filming some clouds with the nose camera, instructing the pilot to fly as straight as possible for around five minutes. Since we would speed up the footage later and wanted our gameplay levels to last a minute, we figured that would be safe. Still, we were guessing.

Learjets tend to be pretty maneuverable—more so than my stomach was expecting. It only took a few sharp twists and turns during the flight to make me realize I would never have made it as an astronaut. I got motion sickness big time, while Dennis and everyone else seemed to be just fine. I managed to keep my breakfast inside my body until we had to refuel.

We touched down at the tiniest airport I'd ever seen, in the middle of nowhere. Seriously, it was like a small shack surrounded by pavement and runways. Luckily the shack had a small convenience store where, thankfully, they stocked Dramamine. It's worth mentioning that back then, unlike now, there was no such thing as an over-the-counter, non-drowsy version of Dramamine. I knew that taking a pill might knock me out, but I also knew I needed to get back on the plane. I closed my eyes and swallowed the recommended dosage. Once it took effect, the medicine worked well enough to keep my nausea at bay, but as I feared, it also put me into something of a dream-like trance state. Reality seemed just a bit off for the rest of the trip. I remember a lot of it, but it's filtered through a drug-induced haze.

At Lake Powell, the scenery was breathtaking. Even though I was curled up in the back of the plane, woozy and at times barely conscious, I will never forget looking

Some stunning views of Lake Powell, AZ. At times it felt like we were about 30 feet above the water.

out the window and seeing that blue lake and unearthly rock formations around it. Lake Powell is a very popular filming location. They filmed the spaceship crash from the original *Planet of the Apes* there. And we were shooting in absolutely gorgeous, clear-blue-sky weather. Dennis did most of the instructing as to the types of shots we wanted to get, and I chimed in once in a while if I felt there was something I needed to add. At times we flew so low above the water, I thought we would scrape the surface, but I think that was just an illusion. Or a symptom of my Dramamine-induced stupor. We found out weeks later that, even though we were flying fast and low, the footage seemed slow and we needed to speed it up considerably to get the effect we wanted.

On the way back from Arizona, we picked up some shots of sandy deserts and farmland, explaining that we wanted the horizon to be just at the top of the frame. This proved a bit tricky at first, but they finally got the hang of it. Eventually, we started to lose light and needed to get back. The one shot we couldn't get was a fly-by over the Hollywood sign; we couldn't get permission to fly the jet over Los Angeles proper. Our L.A. producers would get that shot later via helicopter. Still, it was a very productive day and we left California feeling that our producers understood what we needed, and would be able to get it without us being there.

With our mission in California completed, we went back to Chicago, where there was no shortage of work to be done. We set our sights on the story scenes. This meant hiring actors and a production company that could accommodate our sets. Once again, someone did the research and found a local studio willing to take on our project. I was just thrilled that I wouldn't have to do any stunt flying again. That relief would not last.

AUDITIONS AND INTERSTITIALS

I remember the auditions very well, although I had nothing to do with setting them up other than bringing in some actors I knew. I'd been taking an acting class outside of work and was also part of a sketch comedy group with some friends from an earlier improv class, so I invited my actor friends to audition. But there were also a lot of people who auditioned that I didn't know and had no idea where they'd come from. I credit Rich Tracy (in producer mode) for hiring a local casting director. At any rate, we tried to polish up the script as best we could in preparation, and chose scenes for the actors to read.

One thing I haven't yet mentioned was the idea of doing "interstitials"—super-short scenes that would appear in the middle of a level to show something happening on the ground (usually for a laugh, or at least a chuckle) while the fighters and aliens flew overhead. The concept was not mine, and I remember feeling some resistance to it, for the same reason I had objected to changing camera angles mid-level. I liked the idea but felt it would be disorienting. From a practical standpoint, I wondered what would happen if you fired a shot that was about to hit an enemy ship, only to have the game cut away. But I was in the minority. Everyone else thought it was a great idea, so we all agreed to try it. If it didn't work, we could always remove them.

We wrote a bunch of interstitial gags specific to each level, and gave some of them to the actors who came in to audition. The auditions took place in a small office room. I think all of the design team was present and perhaps a couple of others. Actors came in one by one and depending on their look, we asked them to try out for specific roles. A lot of what we asked the actors to do was non-verbal. I think I asked pretty much every actor who came in to look up and react as if there were alien ships flying across the sky. There was a lot of horrified screaming going on that day. It was almost as ridiculously surreal as the meeting where Q*bert got his name.

But we found our actors. Among our principal characters were the crew members in the control room, the president of the United States, and our villainous general. The most important role was our lead, the commander in the control room. I was rooting for a friend from my acting class, John Hadlestadt. I thought he was perfect. He was an actor and model with leading-man good looks and a Robert Stack type of persona. At the auditions, no one else came close, and John became our hero, Captain Tracy. The rest of our lead actors were people we'd just met at the audition. We were especially thrilled with the guy who became our villain. He lent a Shakespearean grandeur to the role and ate up the scenery. The interstitials created many roles to fill, and some actors were chosen from the auditions, but many were handed out to family and friends.

By the way, it turned out that once the game was on test, many players thought the interstitials were one of the highlights of the game. I'm happy to admit when I'm wrong.

THE LIVE-ACTION SHOOT

Even before the shoot began, I knew I wanted to be the one to edit all the LaserDisc footage. My reasons were selfish. As a teenager in Brooklyn, I'd made Super-8 films with my friend, Ivan. Some I directed, and some he did. And though I had no acting aspirations in my youth, I loved monster movies and was fascinated with how makeup could transform an actor into a monster. So I bought a Dick Smith Monster Makeup Kit and turned myself into Dracula, Wolfman, and the Mummy for our films. When it came time to pick a college, I was equally inclined to pursue a career in either filmmaking or computer engineering. My parents and teachers steered me toward the latter and that was fine by me, but now I had an opportunity to dive back into filmmaking and I wanted that very badly.

What a kick it was to arrive at this small studio in a nondescript building just outside of downtown Chicago and see the sets that had been created for us. The main set, the control room, had only three walls to allow for positioning of the camera, and it looked suitably cheesy without being embarrassingly bad. It was perfect. An additional set was the cockpit of a fighter jet, which was used for all the fighter pilot scenes. Only the back and side of the cockpit were built, leaving it open for the camera to see inside.

I was also impressed by the costumes. Our hero and villain both had military-type uniforms, while the rest of the crew wore jumpsuits. Our color-coded fighter pilots all had helmets that matched the color of their nicknames. Stenciled onto the front of each helmet was the name of someone involved in the creation of the game. Rich Tracy was in his element here, creating each pilot's headgear from a motorcycle helmet with a hose affixed to one side.

Despite my status as a wannabe filmmaker, the production company already had a director who was familiar with his crew and the camera they were using. As filming began (or, more accurately, videotaping, as the control room scenes and interstitials were shot with a studio-quality video camera), the production company director called all the shots, literally. But they weren't exactly the kind of shots I was hoping for. They looked kind of static and uninteresting. I was looking for something approaching a *Star Wars* feel, and what we were getting was more *Plan 9 from Outer Space*. Also, this director had a tendency to move on without giving the actors any notes. If an actor's delivery was a little more relaxed than it should be in a tense, life-or-death "aliens are attacking" situation, he never suggested that they raise the stakes. So I felt an obligation, as one of the game's designers and the person who was going to edit all of this together, to . . . well, sort of stick my nose in. I felt a little bad about doing this at first, but I knew the tone I wanted and we weren't getting it.

At first, I just went over and had a quiet conversation with the director after each shot. "Can you lower the camera a little and try to get a more dramatic angle from below?" "Can you have that actor be a little more nervous when he says that?" And so on. He was very amenable (after all, we were paying for this), so I continued to get bolder in asking for what I thought we needed. Our discussions became longer and after a while, he stopped trying to set up shots without asking me first what I wanted. Eventually, he stopped talking to the actors entirely and pretty much just let me direct them. He and the cameraman were helpful in guiding me through what shots were and weren't possible, given the kind of video camera and lens we were using. We eventually fell into a groove and got the shots and performances we needed.

Special kudos goes to the actor who played the president of the United States. As I mentioned before, if a player gets to the end of the game, the president delivers a speech praising them for their courage and bravery, and then instructs them on how to enter their initials into the high score table. The actor's delivery was perfect: dry and dead serious. One second, he's describing a grateful nation saluting its champion. Then, without skipping a beat, he's telling you to use the joystick to select letters. It's so incongruous that to this day, I cannot watch that speech without laughing.

Some tidbits of trivia: In the *American Gothic* interstitial, the farmer is Dave Faust. One of the control room crew actors, Gregory Franklin, also appeared in a couple of interstitials—as Clark Kent in one scene, and as a trenchcoat-wearing flasher in another. Five of the names on the pilots' helmets were of the following Gottlieb employees: Davis, Faust, Nordman, Lee, and Browne (for Boyd Browne, president of Mylstar), as were the names of the hero, Captain Tracy, and the villain, General Waxman. The sixth pilot, Gabrius, was named for the production company director. And I was onscreen playing fighter pilot Mean Green (wearing the green helmet that says Davis), although I didn't do the voice of Mean Green. For some reason, I voiced White Knight instead.

THE FOREST

Return of the Jedi had just been released that summer. Dennis had a particular fondness for the forest chase scene in it, and wanted one of our levels to have a similar chase. As it turned out, Dave Faust knew of a park in Kalamazoo, Michigan, called the Al Sabo Land Preserve, where trees were planted in rows. He felt it would make a perfect shooting location for us.

Obviously if you're zooming through a forest, you're going to need to avoid hitting trees. So my plan was for the forest level to start like a normal first-third person level, with a viewpoint directly behind the fighter jet. Then, after a while, some trees wouldn't pass by you. They would grow to take up a portion of the screen and linger for a few frames. If you didn't swerve or roll away from it, you crashed and lost some energy. To accomplish this, my code would have to track objects on the LaserDisc from frame to frame, as *M.A.C.H. 3* did with their bombing targets. But that work would come later, after the footage had been shot and edited.

Before we could go out to Kalamazoo and shoot the forest footage, we needed a cameraman. No one internally at Gottlieb had that skill. Fortunately, Rich Tracy, again acting as producer, found a guy who had apparently worked on some of the big budget films recently shot in Chicago. Not only that, but there was a recent advancement in camera technology that allowed a cameraman to strap a camera onto his body and move without creating the jittery footage typical with hand-held filming. It was called the Steadicam, and this cameraman, Greg Lundsgaard, owned one of the only rigs in Chicago. He was our man.

Winter was approaching and our deadline creeping ever closer as we drove the 2 ½ hours from Chicago to Kalamazoo. This time, Dave Faust and Rich Tracy were present, but Dennis was not. Greg brought a crew of two, consisting of an assistant and the assistant's girlfriend. We set up in a motel and got a good night's sleep before heading out to the nearby forest.

We checked in at the ranger station first, and then moved into the forest to start shooting. I'd never seen a Steadicam before, and it was an amazing rig—a set of interconnected spring arms that transferred the weight of the camera to the harness in a way that allowed the camera to seem to float in position. Greg knew what he was doing, and Rich, Dave, and I just watched in awe. In fact, Greg had an enormous confidence. No shot was too difficult, no obstacle too insurmountable.

We did a variety of runs through the forest—walking, jogging, running. We mounted the camera high, then mounted it low. I had Greg do some shots where he'd run up to a particular tree and stop, so that the tree filled a specific part of the frame. I'd need those as targets for the player to avoid. At one point, Greg strapped himself to the hood of his truck and shot while his assistant drove the truck along an access road adjacent to the forest. As it was late in the year, the ground was completely covered in snow. The cold just motivated us to keep moving and get what we needed.

Filming trees in Kalamazoo, MI. This was our first time working with Steadicam operator Greg Lundsgaard. We spent two days roaming the Alsabo Land Preserve. Greg stopped at nothing to get us what we wanted, including getting tied to the hood of a car and shooting while it was being driven down a road.

We'd planned for two days of shooting in the forest, so after a productive first day, we headed back to the motel. Greg decided we needed to see dailies of what we shot, but I thought that seemed impossible on so many levels. How could we get the film processed in Kalamazoo? And even if we did, where could we watch dailies? We didn't have a screening room or film projector handy. But nothing was ever impossible to Greg. He just acted as if whatever he needed would be made available to him. And he was pretty much right.

Greg made a few phone calls until he found a delivery service that could take our film back to Chicago. Then he arranged with a lab in Chicago to have it processed overnight and delivered back to us in the morning. But even with reels of developed 16mm film in our hands, how were we going to view it? Greg once again picked up the phone and began calling local movie theaters, asking to speak to the manager. He explained that we were in town shooting a movie (he didn't elaborate, so it seemed as if it were a big Hollywood film) and needed a place to

While filming in Kalamazoo, Steadicam operator Greg sweet-talked the manager of this movie theater into letting us watch our dailies before the theater opened.

watch our dailies. It took maybe three phone calls before he found a manager willing to turn a theater over to us.

And so, at around ten o'clock the following morning, we showed up at the Plaza 2 Theatres with a couple of reels of film that had just been delivered to our motel. The kind manager was absolutely thrilled to be helping us out, which I could only attribute to his assuming we were some big Hollywood movie-makers. We were given a tour of the projection booth and watched an employee thread our film onto the projector. Then we were ushered into a completely empty theater where, before long, our footage appeared on the huge screen to an audience of three: Greg, Dave Faust, and myself.

Watching the footage was as helpful as Greg had said it would be. After seeing what was working well and what needed to be adjusted, we returned to the forest armed with that new knowledge, and shot some more before heading home. As a result of the footage we got, I ended up putting two forest levels in the game—the first of them being much easier by virtue of having fewer trees to possibly crash into.

Creating Q*bert

THE WINDY CITY

But as fate would have it, we weren't quite done with Greg. Although our L.A. producers were flying to different places, gathering footage for us, one place they didn't need to visit was our own backyard—Chicago! We had no intention of leaving our great city out of the alien invasion; we just had to shoot that footage ourselves. Once again, the arrangements seemed to happen magically, and on a bitterly cold winter morning, I found myself at Meigs Field near Lake Michigan, standing next to a helicopter being prepped to take Dennis, myself, Greg, and his assistant into the skies above Chicago.

We almost didn't make it, though. The temperature with the wind-chill factor was well below zero, and we had some problems getting the camera to operate. It didn't help that the side door of the helicopter was open and Greg was literally hanging out of it. Seriously! He was attached to the helicopter and the camera by what looked like a mountain-climbing strap, while the camera itself was attached to the side with a seriously heavy-duty

Our second shoot with Greg found us in a helicopter over Chicago in below freezing temperatures.

The camera was mounted to the open helicopter side door, and Greg was strapped to both the helicopter and the camera. We flew all over Chicago with Greg hanging out of the helicopter like that.

piece of mounting hardware. Dennis and I took turns sitting in front with the pilot, where there was a heater providing some warmth to our feet. Still, I spent most of that day unable to feel my toes at all.

The footage we got was amazing. We flew north and south, getting shots of the Chicago skyline. We flew west, then turned around and got footage of the city as downtown got closer and closer. We flew south and then followed the Chicago River back all the way into downtown, where somehow we'd gotten permission to fly low amidst the skyscrapers. All because we were making a movie, apparently. It was incredible.

Although the cold was pretty near unbearable, and I still felt a mild degree of motion sickness, my discomfort was trivial compared to what Greg must have gone through that day, hanging out of the side of the chopper. This guy had balls of steel, and his example stayed with me from then on. To be clear, I'm not saying I suddenly developed balls of steel, but in situations where I might

Left: Screen shot from *Pro-Vid-Guard-Argus*, with the bulldozer clearing rubble at the bottom.

Middle: The "Waxman" marquee for the comical version of *Pro-Vid-Guard-Argus*. (Artwork by Jeff Lee.)

Bottom: This was a wondrous sight to behold. Seeing rows of *Q*bert*'s being built on the assembly line was surreal for me.

This is the only picture I have of myself developing *Q*bert*. Note the plastic bucket housing the joystick. This was after the move to Northlake, but before we switched over to IBM PC's as evidenced by the presence of the Blue Box. I'm guessing the playfield was upside down because I was working on the cocktail version of the game, where players sit head-to-head over a screen that faces directly up. The playfield has to rotate 180 degrees for each player's turn.

Flyer for *Q*bert*'s appearance at the November 1982 AMOA show.

This is the cover of *Video Games* magazine featuring the article by Neil Tesser about *Q*bert* and *Joust*. Since Gottlieb didn't want our identities revealed, Jeff, Dave, and I were referred to as R.Teeste, J. Walkman, and D. Ziner respectively.

Above: Marketing brochure showing licensed products.

Below: Two variations on *Q*bert*'s control panel art. The photo on top is from my engineering sample cabinet, which is a Frankenstein of different parts. The photo below is from a production cabinet. Notice how the title of the game on the engineering sample is "@!#?!@" and that the production cabinet added a rule about staying on the pyramid. The drawing of Q*bert himself is also different from one control panel to the other.

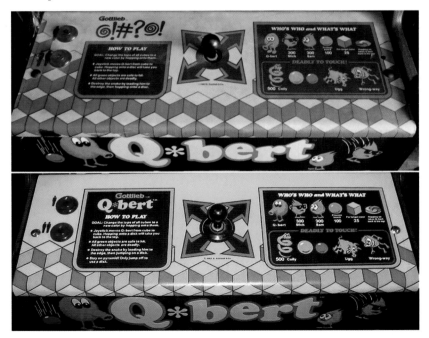

Above: From an unknown Sunday newspaper, a Hi-C-related *Q*bert* Sweepstakes from 1984.

Below: A giveaway of the specially created Mello Yello version of *Q*bert*. I wish I knew who won that!

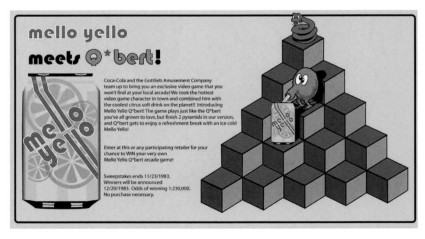

Creating Q*bert

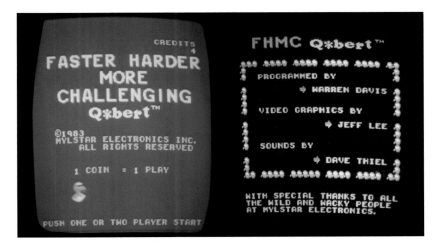

Above: *FHMC Q*bert* title screen on the left. On the right, the credits screen we were allowed to put into *FHMC Q*bert* after the backlash from the *Video Games* magazine article.

Below: Screen shot from the intro to the bonus round in *FHMC Q*bert*. Notice the extension of Q*bert's nose, which managed to make the Coca-Cola executives nervous when we suggested doing that for the Mello Yello version.

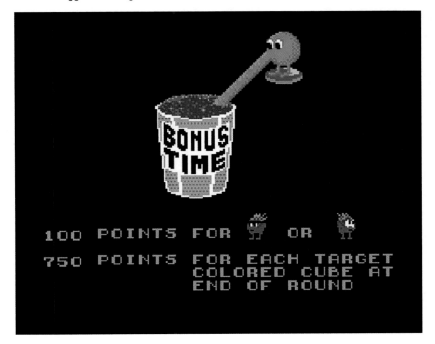

Us vs. Them flyer, back side, showing the wide variety of types of gameplay, story scenes, and interstitials.

Above: Behind the scenes during the control room shoot for *Us vs. Them*.

Below: Gottlieb's Art Director Rich Tracy (left) confers with Dennis Nordman and the actor playing General Waxman.

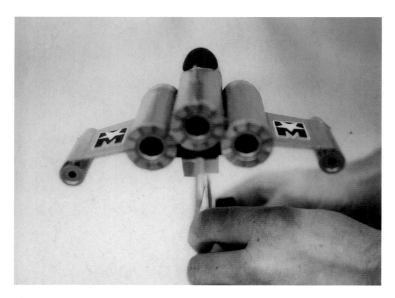

Above: Polaroid reference photo of the model Jeff made for *Us vs. Them* of the player's fighter jet, complete with tiny Mylstar logos on the wings. From photos like these, he would hand-create every image of the plane we would need, pixel by pixel, using FOGUS (our foreground sprite tool).

Below: A screen shot showing the alien mothership.

Above: I got really excited about doing a pseudo-3D version of *Blockade* (which was the original version of the light cycle game in *Tron*). Doing it on sprite-based 2D hardware was challenging, but it looked cool. The playfield was bigger than the screen and the view scrolled. Ultimately, though, it proved to be impractical.

Below: Another attempt at a pseudo-3D game with multiple copies of the spaceship at different sizes used to give the illusion of depth. Again, it looked cool, but there was no real game there and I gave up on it pretty quickly.

An ad for home versions of *Q*bert*. Ported by Parker Bros. to eight home gaming platforms.

A flyer for *Lotto Fun*, a ticket dispensing game made on Williams hardware. The idea came from Howie Rubin, who hired Jeff Lee to do the artwork and me to do the programming.

Creating Q*bert

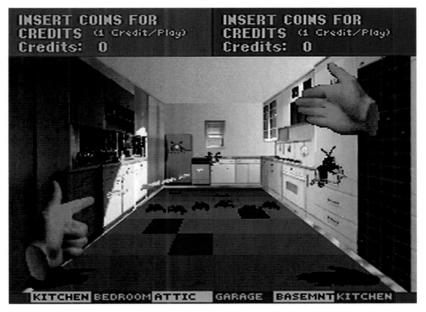

A gameplay screen shot from *Exterminator*. The left hand is shooting while the right hand is about to avoid getting stung by a wasp.

Above: The *Exterminator* "tease" cabinet on the show floor at the Las Vegas Hilton.

Left: An *Exterminator* cabinet sitting in our Las Vegas suite to show to select distributors during the 1989 ACME show. Every time the game was played was a harrowing experience, wondering if it would freeze from noise issues during gameplay. Luckily most distributors didn't play it long enough for the problem to surface. Not all, but most.

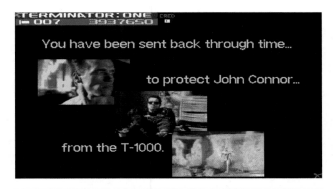

Top: Fun with compression algorithms! These are some of the digitized movie clips that were used in the *T2* arcade game.

Middle: If you enter my initials and birthday into *NBA Jam Tournament Edition*, you'll be able to play using my name and head. (I think there are about 50 or so Williams employees' heads in the game.)

Botttom: I also make a (very) brief appearance in *Revolution X* as the guy who ducks under the desk and lobs grenades at you. You can't shoot me, but you can shoot the chains holding up the Evergreen Chemical sign.

Top: *The Revolution X* team photo:
Top row (left to right): Designer and Lead Programmer George Petro, artist John Vogel, Designer and Lead Artist Jack Haeger, Steven Tyler, programmer Bill Dabelstein, Joe Perry, artists John Newcomer and Steve Beran. • Bottom row (left to right): Sound designer Chris Granner, artist Marty Martinez, and myself (with Steven Tyler's hand on my back). Yes—he touched me.

Middle: *Revolution X* is introduced at the 1993 AMOA show.

Botttom: Engineering tech Sheridan Oursler playing submissive with Kerri Hoskins as Mistress Helga while other *Revolution X* characters watch.

Creating Q*bert

have been afraid or doubtful of achieving a goal, remembering Greg's confidence and attitude would inspire me to forge ahead and not give up so easily.

MUSIC

Another pleasant surprise from management had to do with musical accompaniment for the game. Our hardware's soundboard had been revised since *Q*bert*'s release, but it still provided only crude synthesized sound. Craig Bierwaltes, *Us vs. Them*'s sound designer, did the best he could with that hardware. But since we had a LaserDisc player, that meant we had the ability to mix actual recorded music onto the soundtrack. Another one of our sound designers, Dave Zabriskie, had a background in composing music and was very excited about doing a full orchestral, John Williams-like score. This could have been recorded on a high-end synthesizer in his office, but amazingly, management approved the hiring of a small live orchestra and studio time. Dave took on the challenge and created a phenomenal score for the game from start to finish, recorded with an orchestra of about a dozen musicians.

EDITING

In addition to programming chores, I took on the responsibility of editing all the live action and flying footage we'd acquired, having convinced management that my high school filmmaking experiences somehow qualified me for this task. It may have been partly true, but mostly I wanted the experience of editing those live-action sequences. And as editor, I could determine where the interstitial gags would be placed within each level, and how long they would last.

For *M.A.C.H. 3*, Gottlieb had purchased what at the time was a pretty sweet editing system, based on the Sony U-Matic video format. This format used ¾-inch tape housed in a cassette that was slightly larger than a VHS tape. There were two U-Matic player/recorders, each with its own TV monitor and a controller that connected the two. One of the U-Matic machines played the source material, and the other contained the assembled edit. The room where this system resided became my home away from home.

The live-action control room footage became available to us as soon as we finished shooting it, and the flying footage from our original trip to L.A. had already been delivered and converted to video. But the rest of the footage from our L.A. producers came in more slowly. I needed to turn each edited level over to Dave Zabriskie for scoring, but the actual recording of the music couldn't happen until every level was scored (so we would only have to hire the orchestra once). The sheer amount of work to be done was enormous. I pulled a few all-nighters to get the control room scenes done, resting for a bit before coming back to do more programming during the day.

Flying footage came in gradually, and most of it was great. Our producers went to Hawaii, where they got some great footage of beaches and Diamond Head. They also shot in San Francisco and around the Golden Gate Bridge. They even rented a helicopter to get us a beautiful shot over the L.A. Basin, which culminated in that fly-by we wanted of the Hollywood sign. The helicopter footage turned out to be a lot more jittery than the Learjet footage, which was only exaggerated further by speeding it up. Thankfully, there was one usable take. We never did get the Statue of Liberty or Mount Rushmore, but we didn't have time to get misty over it.

With our February deadline looming, December and January became a blur. My belief in this project was so strong, I became somewhat obsessed with getting it completed on time. The game didn't really require much in the way of sprites or sounds, so the burden of completion fell on my shoulders. At some point, it became obvious that there was just too much to do. Not only did each level of gameplay need to be edited, but some levels had two or three different options to prepare. Plus the mothership levels, forest levels, and final battle inside the mothership all had unique gameplay that had to be coded. High score initials entry needed to be programmed, and the operator diagnostics code needed to be customized for this game.

Once the LaserDisc footage was locked, it would take some time to send it out and have test LaserDiscs burned. And if there were any problems with the test burn, we'd have to fix our source material and send it out again. There just wasn't enough time to take that risk for the entire game.

So we devised a plan to put together an abbreviated version of the game to reduce the workload. It would be missing the later levels and the ending, but it would give attendees of the A.O.E. show a sense of what the game would be. Making the deadline still wasn't a certainty, but I was determined to do it. I worked crazy hours, driven by my stubborn and even selfish desire to see people play this game. Maybe part of me was driven by wanting another taste of my previous success. I certainly believed, naively perhaps, that this game could be as popular as Q*bert if not more so.

Days flew by. The limited number of levels that needed editing were edited, the score was recorded, the preliminary LaserDiscs were burned, and somehow, it looked like all of my efforts would pay off. I'd been working furiously, and it would certainly come down to the wire, but by some miracle it looked like I'd be able to have something ready to show on the convention center floor.

And then the rug got pulled out from under me.

With only a few days until the AOE, Frank Ballouz came over to my cubicle and gravely let me know that *Us vs. Them* would not be going to the upcoming show. I tried to convince him that everything would be ready and functional in time, but he said it didn't matter. The decision had been made. Bringing an incomplete game to a show was risky enough, but to bring one that hadn't been on location testing (and therefore had no coin-test results) and might not even be ready in time (despite my assurances) was apparently a risk that upper management couldn't stomach. I had to wonder if Howie would have made the same call, but of course there was no way to know.

I was crushed. It didn't help that I'd been running on adrenaline for weeks now with one and only one goal in mind. Suddenly, that goal was ripped from me. And although Frank tried to have me look on the bright side, saying, "Look, now you can slow down and finish the game at a normal pace," I didn't see it that way. It felt like I'd been robbed of something. I no longer had a purpose. It occurred to me that without some good buzz from the AOE, *Us vs. Them* wouldn't get the publicity or traction it might need to succeed.

I didn't know what to do. I went home and stayed there for a couple of days.

When I returned, still bitter but somewhat refreshed, I set about finishing what remained to be done. The AOE came and went without *Us vs. Them* and I forged on, working a normal 9-to-5 schedule. I edited the remaining levels, coded what needed to be coded, and a month or so later, we had a game to test.

Creating Q*bert

TESTING

In-house testing had been going on while the game was being developed, but now it was time for field-testing. All the elements of our *M.A.C.H. 3* replacement kit were prepared, including cabinet side art by artist Larry Day featuring a large frightened face in the crowd that looked remarkably like Jeff Lee. An *Us vs. Them* cabinet was delivered to an arcade and left there for a few weeks. Each week we got coin collection results back from the arcade owner. Each week the test results were the same—number one! The game was the top earner in that arcade week after week!

We placed another *Us vs. Them* on test at another location, and the results were similar. Management was thrilled. All of us on the design team were thrilled. All indications were that we had another hit on our hands. It seemed like cause for celebration.

Armed with the results from the coin tests, our sales department reached out to distributors, who were only too eager to place orders for this new mega-hit. The future looked so bright for this title that Gottlieb was able to obtain orders for new *Us vs. Them* cabinets and prepared the production line to start building them. All of the time, effort, and money the company had sunk into this game was going to pay off. The debacle of the AOE seemed a distant memory.

But there were new debacles on the horizon that signaled a bleak future not only for *Us vs. Them*, but for the video game industry in general. The promise and potential of LaserDisc arcade games was about to come to a screeching halt.

CHAPTER SEVEN

GOTTLIEB'S DEMISE

As Gottlieb's sales department took orders for *Us vs. Them,* a backlash against LaserDisc games was brewing and would soon come to a head. Inside every LaserDisc game (not just ours) was a particular model LaserDisc player made by Pioneer, and apparently it was not ready for prime time.

Pinball machines tend to take a pounding. Playing them inspires a degree of excitement, perhaps anger if a shot is missed or a ball is lost. It's not uncommon for people to slam a machine when that happens. Video games are not all that different. When you're playing a game and not having a very good time of it, you might kick the machine or push it. And with a game consisting solely of solid-state components, that wouldn't be a problem. But those LaserDisc players sitting inside video game cabinets were particularly susceptible to being jarred.

The way that data on a LaserDisc is read is not unlike a phonograph needle on a vinyl album; it can skip and lose sync, meaning the game loses track of what frame is playing. But the game software is dependent on that sync. Without it, the game gets confused and can't continue. The player sees a blank or jumbled screen suddenly, and they can kiss their quarter or fifty cents or whatever they paid goodbye.

At this point, the player hunts down the nearest

arcade employee, who has to reset the machine and give the player their money back. Not good. The arcade owner is eventually going to hear about it and, not surprisingly, they will be unhappy about it. If it happens too much, they might even complain to their distributor. When distributors learn that a game has problems, orders for that game will most likely stop. Maybe some existing orders will be canceled.

Now consider this. When word gets out among players that banging or shoving a LaserDisc game will allow them to get their money back, regardless of how long they've been playing it, well . . . some players just might do that on purpose. After a while, arcade operators might turn the game off, so it's just taking up space on the arcade floor without earning any money. And if the problem persists, that game will most likely be replaced with another game that doesn't have that problem.

This is essentially what happened to LaserDisc video games in 1984—not just Gottlieb/Mylstar's, but those made by all manufacturers. The Pioneer player couldn't withstand the abuse it got in the arcades, and the game cabinets just weren't engineered to absorb that kind of impact. The response from operators and distributors alike was that the technology was faulty. It was a fad, they concluded, and it was time to go.

It's probably worth noting that while pinball machines had a "tilt" sensor to lock the game if a player tried lifting the cabinet (to influence the ball), this wouldn't have helped a LaserDisc game, since it was the vibrations from banging the side that caused the problem. I'm not sure if there were cost-effective vibration sensors at the time. I'm guessing there weren't, but I'm not sure anyone ever thought something like that would be needed.

For Mylstar, this meant that some big orders for *Us vs. Them* were canceled. They had ramped up their production line to supply those orders, and the games were already being built. So management felt they had no choice but to file a lawsuit against their own distributors. The rationale was that those orders represented a contract to take possession of *Us vs. Them* cabinets and kits, and Mylstar had spent time and money in good faith to deliver them.

I didn't follow the lawsuit closely, and I'm not sure of the details of the outcome. What mattered to me was that the production line had stopped abruptly as Mylstar scrambled to get rid of whatever remaining cabinets they'd built. It was a disaster for the company to be sure, but similar stories could be found throughout the coin-op video game industry. It wouldn't have mattered if the technical issues were solved that very moment. The word "LaserDisc" became tainted, synonymous with failure. LaserDiscs in video games were dead.

I don't know how many dedicated *Us vs. Them* machines went out the door. Probably under a thousand, which makes them very rare nowadays. But it taught me a couple of valuable lessons about the marketplace: 1) it can be very fickle, and 2) success or failure isn't always in your control.

Regardless, I loved the experience of making this game, with all its highs and lows, pressures, and victories. Of all my work in the video game industry, this may be the game I'm most proud of. When I look back at what we did, it seems completely impossible that was done within a budget that Gottlieb considered reasonable. We had actors, we had sets, we had costumes, we had orchestral music, we had special effects (cheesy though they may have been). And we had all of that flying footage. That all had to cost money, yet to this day I still have no idea how much.

But man, what a great time we had.

Despite the way things turned out, I never thought the future of the company was in jeopardy. Ignorance is bliss sometimes. I don't think any of us realized it then, but the party was basically over.

ONWARD AND DOWNWARD

With *Us vs. Them* firmly behind me, I found myself suffering a bit from PTSD. The small number of *Us vs. Them* games produced was a devastating blow to me. My motivation for making any game was to entertain people, and to put in all of that work and effort on something that I believed in so strongly, only to have it denied the opportunity to be seen and played, was tough to swallow. The fact that it tested so well and seemed to be headed towards success only compounded my grief. And I suppose the all-nighters and general lack of attention to my well-being began to catch up with me, too.

But as they say in Brooklyn, "Whaddya gonna do?" I gave myself some time to recover and eventually had to move on. The question was: Move on to what? As had happened after *Q*bert*, I was able to expand my field of view after *Us vs. Them* and look at what was going on around me. The company was changing from what it once was, and not necessarily for the better.

I'd been with Gottlieb/Mylstar for over two years, and in that time I'd come to believe I could be happy there for the rest of my life. I'm not sure if nowadays any young person imagines they'll stay at a job they love for their entire lifetime, but back then it seemed like a real possibility. I don't think I ever felt that way at Bell Labs. Gottlieb was different. It felt like home. I liked what I was doing and I liked the people I worked with. And despite its ups and downs, I could see myself growing old there, making games until it wasn't fun anymore and then maybe moving on to a management position later in life. What a lovely dream. Not the way it turned out, of course. Things had changed around me during *Us vs. Them*, and I was too busy to fully take it in and understand it.

Howie's departure really cast a shadow on the day-to-day operation of the video department. He and Ron worked very hard to protect us from upper management's needs so we could be creative and innovative without feeling pressured. Howie's energy and support were subtle boosts of inspiration to most of the programmers, even if that didn't always translate into hit games. The staff had grown and there were maybe eight to ten games in various stages of development, but many of them would never see the light of day (although some have been rediscovered in recent years and released to MAME).

The *Us vs. Them* lawsuit left a hole in the production schedule, and it wasn't clear if we had another hit game waiting in the wings. Whether Howie's style of hands-off management—giving programmers complete artistic freedom to pursue any game idea—was at fault for this or not is debatable. Certainly, no one could have foreseen that LaserDiscs would turn out to be a short-lived fad. (Well, maybe they could have, given the unreliability of the Pioneer players in the field, but that's easily said in hindsight.) Despite the LaserDisc situation, the industry itself was changing. The year 1984 would be particularly difficult for all video arcade game manufacturers, because the market was becoming saturated.

It may be difficult to appreciate now, looking at how big the video game industry has become, but the arcade industry exploded in a relatively short period of time. It grew fairly slowly in the 1970s before really accelerating at the end of that decade. Arcades then opened up all over the place, creating a need for games to fill them.

Along with that, video games started appearing in bowling alleys, gas stations, convenience stores, and bars, too. Small manufacturing companies sprang up to cash in on the fad, producing derivative and sub-par games just to make a quick buck. For a while it seemed that you could throw a game anywhere and it would collect quarters. But that kind of growth was unsustainable.

At some point, there were more video games available to play than there were players. And video games were no longer the unique and exciting technology they once were. Some people just got tired of them, or became more discerning as to which games they played. The home video game systems became better, too, giving players close to arcade-quality graphics in the comfort of their homes. As manufacturers pumped out games that didn't collect as much, the distributors stopped buying as many. The result was that the video arcade game industry crashed in 1984.

But when Frank Ballouz replaced Howie in 1983, no one knew this lay ahead. Frank's obligation was to make sure we had a steady stream of games to keep the production line moving. But Howie's style of giving the programmers creative freedom wasn't going to guarantee that. Especially not with the current lineup of programmers.

As the staff had grown, it became apparent that there was some dead weight in the group. Most were very capable programmers. A very few were not. But even those who were had a hard time coming up with marketable game concepts. A lot of games were being developed, but not a lot were progressing to the level of field-testing, and those that did weren't testing well.

And so, to combat what upper management must have believed was a complete lack of structure, they brought in a middle manager to oversee the programmers. His name was Bill Adams.

Bill came from Bally/Midway and was involved in the development of such hit games as *Tron* and *Spy Hunter*. At Mylstar, though, he wasn't hired as a programmer but as a manager, and he had some strict philosophies about how games should be developed. For one thing, he believed it shouldn't take more than four months to finish a game. In contrast, Howie never gave anyone a deadline, although he might come by and ask, "Hey, when do you think we can put this on the schedule?" or "When will this be ready for testing?" Under Bill's regime, programmers were no longer allowed to explore ideas without management approval. Game designs had to be written up and pitched to management, who needed to approve a game and put it on the schedule before a programmer could begin work.

This was a bitter pill for most of our staff. Although in fairness, I don't think it affected me as much as my colleagues. Having been responsible for one of the company's biggest successes, I was given a little more leeway than many of the other programmers who hadn't yet released any game. And I didn't really feel I'd have much difficulty complying with Bill's notion of a four-month development cycle, since *Q*bert* had only taken about four months to get ready for testing. *Us vs. Them* had taken longer, but there had been the added workload of overseeing the flying footage, shooting the live-action scenes, and editing all of the video together.

Still, I was concerned about our ability to make unique, groundbreaking games within that time frame. Experimentation was a key part of my design process, and that carried with it a risk of moving in a wrong direction. If that happened, some re-working might be necessary to get back on track. Those missteps ate up time, but I believed they were worth it in the long run. The new development process didn't really allow for that.

Not that I worried about it much. I will admit to having a certain amount of confidence that I could do whatever I wanted and the company wouldn't fire me. My track record provided me that protection. The same could be said of Chris Brewer and Fred Darmstadt, who were responsible for *M.A.C.H. 3*, and to a lesser degree, Kan Yabumoto, whose *Mad Planets* kept the assembly line moving for a while. And even though *Us vs. Them* wasn't a success, I felt no responsibility for that. I had done my part and was proud of the way it turned out. The circumstances of its failure were truly out of my control. And management knew that.

However, the rest of the programming staff couldn't help but feel resentful of this new way of working. An atmosphere of fear arose in which people worried about losing their jobs if they couldn't come up with a releasable game, and quickly. By the way, "releasable" became our only goal for a game. "Innovative" or "popular" were not considered important objectives. From a business standpoint, I understood the reasoning behind it, but it bothered me that we were churning out product for no reason other than to keep the assembly line moving. Still, I was determined to maintain my own personal standards within this new system. And if for some reason I needed more than four months, I genuinely believed it would be given to me. Sadly, I never got to find out if that were true.

THE FINAL DAYS

I had to pitch my next project just like everybody else. This was a new thing for me. My process up to that point involved playing around with an idea and letting it evolve. I had no idea how to plan out an entire game in advance. Still, confident in the security of my job, I decided not to worry about it. I wrote up a bunch of ideas and described them to the best of my ability. In truth, I had no intention of sticking to those descriptions if I got inspired to go off in a different direction.

I have a copy of my pitch memo from July 1984. It involves descriptions of such stellar concepts as "Space Mason" and "Fort Knox 2900 AD," two somewhat lame attempts to name a game before programming it, as well as the more generically named "Hands" and "The Wall." "Hands" was a pitch for the fly-catching game that I'd already programmed for internal use, and "The Wall" was a pseudo-3D version of the old game Block-ade, a concept that had later been re-purposed by Bally into *Tron*'s Light Cycle game. To do that in pseudo-3D on our 2D sprite-based hardware would have been pretty impressive. I actually spent some time exploring it and it looked great, but there were problems I couldn't solve and I eventually dropped it. As I expected, I took no flak from management over that.

As the year dragged on, the morale in the department began to decline. The industry-wide slump gradually be-came apparent to us, and the future looked uncertain. Summer came to an end, and there was a strange feel-ing of somberness throughout the department. Whereas there used to be a lot of laughter and people having fun, the office started to seem quiet and reserved. People talk-ed in hushed tones, making sure others weren't listening. I myself began to dread coming to work—something I never thought possible. I realized that I could no longer see myself working for this company for decades into the future.

That realization brought a valuable life lesson to me. We live in a world of instability and change. When things are good, it's best to be prepared for the eventu-ality that it may not last. If things stay good—well, great, that's a welcome surprise. But it will always help you to appreciate what you have if you at least acknowledge the possibility that it could all vanish in an instant.

One of the bright spots of this generally dark time was meeting John Newcomer, who'd come to Gottlieb in the midst of the industry downturn. As with other non-programmer designers, I think he floundered in Gottlieb's programmer-centric culture. Not that it mattered, as things turned out.

There came a time when I think everyone knew that something was up, although many (including me) didn't know exactly what. Word got around that some bigwigs from Coca-Cola, our corporate overlords for the last couple of years, were meeting with upper management in the front office. If anyone up there knew what was happening, they either kept quiet or shared it with very few others. The strange feeling of foreboding became more and more palpable every day. It's a feeling I've not experienced anywhere else I've ever worked. Everyone could sense it. We couldn't help but talk about it, quietly and in private, but we didn't know just exactly what was in store. A management upheaval? The shutting down of the pinball department? Speculation was rampant, but we just went through the motions of doing our jobs.

Finally, the answer came. Shortly after I arrived at the office one morning, Ron Waxman stepped into our large work area, which was filled with cubicles and outlined by private offices, and made an announcement in a loud booming voice, like the voice of God.

"Ladies and gentlemen, please stop working. We are closed. Mylstar is officially shutting down."

This was a surreal moment and hard to process. As much as working there had become joyless and oppressive, I don't think I was prepared for something this drastic. Ron continued to announce that we would all be meeting individually with a severance specialist to go over the terms of Mylstar's closure and how it would affect each of us.

It felt like grief counseling.

The terms of the severance were generous, as I recall ... something like eight weeks of pay with continued insurance. They also discussed placement options to get us into other jobs. As unhappy as I was in those final days, this was a lot to take on short notice. The experience left me numb. When we were finished with our severance meetings, we were asked to collect our things and leave. I remember that by the time I left, some programmers had already lined up interviews at other companies. Neil Burnstein was contacted by a headhunter and got an interview with a company called Datalogics that was looking for programmers with graphics experience.

By the way, I should mention that getting calls from headhunters was a pretty commonplace occurrence. It happened to me at every job I've ever had, sometimes more than once a week. At first, it seemed a little odd to me that some stranger would call me at my job to see if I'd be interested in finding another job. But eventually I just accepted it as normal. Usually, I would politely say, "No, thanks," and hang up. Sometimes they'd ask if they could call me back in a few months, and I'd usually say, "Sure." After all, it'd be easy enough to say no again if they called back. I was so happy at Gottlieb, I could never imagine even hearing what other options were out there, but if they wanted to call and get turned down, sure, why not.

Apparently, on the day we were all let go, some headhunter got wind of Gottlieb's demise and trolled for programmers to fill positions for his clients. This was the man who'd contacted Neil Burnstein. He was calling all of our office numbers, one after another. When he called me, I told him I was interested and he set up an interview for me at Datalogics as well.

That interview worked out, and it wasn't long before I was employed again. Datalogics was located in the River North neighborhood of Chicago. Unlike the tourist mecca that it is today, River North was a pretty dismal-looking and underdeveloped industrial area then. No more White Castle nearby for lunch or Entenmann's Discount Bakery, but Al's Beef was just a couple of blocks away. Another perk was that I no longer had to drive to work. I was able to get there on a relatively short L train ride. As a native New Yorker, riding the train was a welcome change from driving out to the suburbs.

Datalogics was a company that had developed some software that was pretty revolutionary for its time. They called it pagination software. Nowadays, we call them word processors. If you can imagine it, the very first version of Microsoft Word had only recently been released, and it wasn't remotely as useful as Datalogics' software, which ran on computers much more powerful than the consumer PCs of that time. And rather than selling their software, Datalogics provided pagination as a service to their clients, who generally needed to maintain very large documents. My job (along with the other new hires) was to add support for graphics—meaning any image stored in some Graphical File Format (or GFF). A lot of GFFs were popping up in those days. The standards of today—like GIF, TIFF, or JPG—hadn't been widely adopted by everyone yet. Instead, it seemed that everybody who wrote software to create or edit graphics was creating their own, sometimes proprietary, GFF for their product. Proprietary meant that a description of the GFF was nowhere to be found, and since my job was to support the inclusion of graphics files within documents, that made my job something of a challenge. And kind of fun.

Rather than think of my new job as a place where old

game programmers go to die, I actually enjoyed my work there. It wasn't making games, but it was a fun office with great people and interesting work. Neil Burnstein had been hired as well, and there was at least one programmer who used to work at Williams—Ken Lantz. Ken had developed Williams' legendary 49-way joystick, first used in *Sinistar*. I missed the world of video games, but I also felt like I'd had my moment there. I'd been given a great opportunity, and I felt like I'd made the most of it. No regrets. Look towards the future, right? Besides, I got out of the video game industry at the right time. The arcade business was imploding. Arcades were closing right and left, and there were fewer games hitting the market. Still, I kept tabs on what was going on in the industry, even if I never actively thought about re-entering it.

Over a year passed at Datalogics and I was still happy as a clam. Okay, maybe "content" would be a better word. But then something unexpected happened. I got a call from a headhunter. Granted, that in itself isn't the unexpected part; as I said, they contacted me periodically. What set this call apart was his opening sentence: "How would you like to get back into video games?" It caught me off-guard. I was so used to brushing off these people, but that sentence stopped me in my tracks. I barely hesitated. "Tell me more," I said. And I was informed that Williams, the maker of such stellar hits as *Defender*, *Joust*, and *Robotron*, was looking to hire. Stunned though I was, I responded instantly. "Yes, get me an interview." It wasn't until that moment that I realized how much I missed that world. And Williams wasn't just any company. For me, it was like the Emerald City, a shining tower. Although I'd heard a little bit about what it was like to work there, warts and all—first from John Newcomer during his short time at Gottlieb, then from Ken Lantz— the thought of being able to continue making games at a company with their track record got me very excited.

The shock must have lasted a while, because I have virtually no memories of the interview process. In my mind, it feels like I hung up the phone and was instantly escorted into my new office at Williams. Obviously, it didn't happen that way, but the details are fuzzy. I do remember feeling terrible about having to quit Datalogics, since everyone there was pretty awesome. And I also remember that they were sympathetic to my decision. I think if any of them had the chance to move into the video game industry, they'd have jumped at it.

I also remember that having made Q*bert gave me a big leg up in getting hired. Apparently, my reputation preceded me. The notion that other people in the industry took note of my success was a little strange for me. You see, I never thought of myself as anyone to particularly take note of. I knew I was appreciated at Gottlieb, but I never really thought anyone at any other company was aware of me at all. And technically they weren't, but they *were* aware of Q*bert. And being the designer/programmer of that game carried a certain cachet. Over the years I've come to accept it, and I'm forever grateful to those who gave me the opportunity to have such a positive reputation. But at the time, especially having been out of the industry for a while, it was a new thing, and it felt good.

In a strange twist worth mentioning, some time later I found out that the headhunter who had gotten me into Datalogics and the headhunter who got me out of there were actually the same person! He used a different name each time because of the murky ethical questions involved with doing that. While I can't say I approve of his methods for bringing me to Williams, I'd have to admit I'm thrilled and grateful that he did.

CHAPTER EIGHT

WILLIAMS AND
THE DAWN OF
DIGITIZATION

I started working at Williams Electronics in March of 1986. My first office there (well, cubicle, actually) was in an area nicknamed "The Dead Zone." This was partially due to its being located about as far in the back of the building as possible, and also because of its isolation from the rest of the offices.

The fluorescents were never on in the Dead Zone, which contained three offices and four cubicles. Two doors on either side of a short walkway connected the Dead Zone with the rest of the building. There were no windows to the outside world, but there were large windows between each office and the walkway. Privacy wasn't welcome in the Dead Zone.

Williams Electronics was located at the corner of California and Roscoe on the northwest side of Chicago, next to the Chicago River. From the outside, the building seemed a bit smaller than Gottlieb's Northlake plant, but the walk to the Dead Zone was surprisingly long. From the main entrance, I'd first pass through the waiting room, where the sweet elderly receptionist would greet me. Then I'd have to briefly cut through the front office area, where people like VP of Engineering Ken Fedesna, VP of Marketing Joe Dillon, noted pinball historian Roger Sharpe, and the company president, Neil Nicastro, had their offices. From there, I'd enter the manufacturing plant.

The plant was home to our assembly lines. There were different lines for pinball and video, although they could be re-configured if necessary. When a line was running, the sound was incredibly loud. When it wasn't, it seemed like a ghost town. The route to my office took me past what seemed like miles of winding metal tracks with partially assembled game cabinets on them, rolling from area to area, getting new parts attached until they were whole. By comparison, at Gottlieb, I could get to my office without ever seeing the assembly lines.

Then I'd go through the abandoned cafeteria (presumably closed when the industry downturn hit), up some stairs, and down a fluorescent-lit hallway flanked by engineering offices that actually had exterior windows, until I reached the door to the Dead Zone.

My cubicle was in the back corner. Adjacent to me was a programmer who was working on *Joust 2* with John Newcomer (designer of the original *Joust*). I don't think the other two cubicles were occupied. Kristina Donofrio, programmer of *Mystic Marathon*, had the center office, but I have no recollection of who were in the other two. They may have been empty for some or all of the time I spent there. Thanks to the recent industry slump, the video department at Williams was pretty close to non-existent.

My first assignment for Williams was to improve their art tools. They were using a program called WIMP (Williams Image Management Program). Not sure who named it that. It was pretty similar to Gottlieb's FO-GUS, in that you'd have a palette of sixteen colors and plop squares of one color into a large grid to create foreground objects. My memories of this work are vague, but I believe I created an exporter for images so they could be included as source code and assembled. Games were written in assembler language, which was very close to the CPU's native binary language but in a (slightly) more readable and understandable form. Every processor had its own assembler language, and while most assembler languages were similar, different manufacturers had their own styles. At Gottlieb, we used Intel CPUs. Williams was big on Motorola, which meant I needed to learn Motorola's assembler language. Before the hardware could run a game, it had to be "assembled" or translated into an "executable," a version that the CPU could run.

Working on art tools got me familiar with Williams' video game system, which was slightly different from Gottlieb's in that there was not a foreground and background plane implemented in hardware. The entire screen was basically a blank canvas, and their game code had to paint everything on that canvas every frame, sixty times a second. To accomplish this, they developed proprietary VLSI (Very Large Scale Integration) integrated circuit chips to "blit," or copy blocks of pixels quickly into screen memory. Their chief hardware designer was Mark Loffredo, a talented guy with a big personality. Mark was fond of a certain saying that has stuck with me to this day. When something went wrong, he would say, "Fuck me in a dog suit!" I think a lot of people at the office picked up on it, and you would occasionally see "FMIADS!" scribbled on walls, Post-Its, memos, or sketchpads.

JOUSTING TIME!

As I mentioned, the video department had been kind of decimated. The crash of '84 had taken its toll on most manufacturers, and Williams was no exception. Some of the programmers who'd been working on video games, such as Larry De Mar (*Defender*, *Stargate*, *Robotron*) or Bill Pfutzenreuter (*Joust*), had been moved over to pinball. I think *Joust 2* was literally the only video game being developed at Williams when I arrived there.

You may well be asking, "Where was Eugene Jarvis?" If you're not familiar with the name, Eugene was largely responsible for putting Williams on the video game map as co-creator (with Larry De Mar) of back-to-back hits *Defender*, *Stargate*, and *Robotron*. Nowadays, he is regarded as a legendary figure in video game history, and rightly so. But even then, he was a superstar. When I learned I'd be working for Williams, I have to confess that I was kind of excited to meet him. I didn't realize he'd left to get his MBA in California.

My boss was Ed Suchocki, manager of the video department. You would think such a small department wouldn't need much managing, but as it turned out, it did. *Joust 2* was falling behind, and the original programmer was let go. Both Kristina Donofrio and I were brought on to finish it.

For those interested in technical details, *Joust 2* used the newly developed System 6 hardware, which was an improved version of the original *Joust*'s System 4. If I recall correctly, the main differences between System 6 and System 4 were an increase in the available memory and a background plane implemented in hardware using fixed size image blocks, much like Gottlieb's hardware. Another of my contributions to WIMP was to support the creation of background art for this new plane, which had its own sixteen-color palette independent of the foreground's.

It was nice to be working with John Newcomer, whom I'd barely gotten to know at Gottlieb before it had closed. And it was exciting to be working on a sequel to *Joust*, a game I felt a minor kinship with since both it and *Q*bert* had been featured in that 1983 *Video Games Magazine* article. And it was challenging to pick things up in the middle of development and try to figure out someone else's code.

Meanwhile, John had his own challenges, due to management's insistence that *Joust 2* be designed for a vertically oriented monitor. You see, *Joust 2* was primarily intended to be sold as a kit—a means of converting a cabinet housing some older game that was past its prime into a brand new game that could hopefully start earning money again. And market research discovered that the games in the field ripest for conversion happened to have vertically oriented monitors. So when *Joust 2* got the green light, it was with the understanding that it would be designed for a vertical monitor.

Fine. Except, of course, that the whole concept of *Joust* involves *jousting*, which requires as much *horizontal* distance as possible. To limit the amount of horizontal space available made no sense, but management is rarely driven by sense so much as cents. They could sell more kits if it played on a vertical monitor, so it was a take-it-or-leave-it situation—and John took it. While I was mildly annoyed that commerce was considered more important than design, it was my job to be a team player and do what I was told. For the most part I enjoyed it, but I also didn't have much of an emotional connection to that game or feel a particular sense of pride about it.

FUN WITH *LOTTO FUN*

After *Joust 2* was done, I went back to art tools. Around that same time, a new opportunity presented itself. Howie Rubin, former VP of Business Development at Gottlieb, had started a new venture on his own based on an idea for a redemption game. These are games that dispense tickets based on your score, which you collect and then trade in at a counter filled with merchandise. There are still lots of arcades today, usually on boardwalks or in "family fun" centers, that have a new generation of redemption games. The "prizes" you can get are about the same as they always were. For maybe fifty tickets, you can get ... a pencil sharpener! Want something cool? Well, that'll cost you about 100,000 tickets or more. Skee-Ball was always my favorite redemption game. Still is, actually.

Anyway, Howie's idea was to have a video game that played like a state lottery. You'd have a choice of how many numbers to pick (three, four, or six), then you'd mark the numbers you wanted on a card. A series of numbered ping-pong balls would then float into a chamber and spin around until the appropriate number of them were randomly sucked out. The digits on the ping-pong balls would be compared to your choices and, based on the results, you'd win a certain number of tickets. Or not. Howie called the game *Lotto Fun*.

It was a simple idea, and easily understood. Howie just needed someone to implement it, since he no longer worked for a game manufacturer. He came to Williams and offered to buy their surplus of old video game hardware boards left over from the crash. In return, they would let Howie "rent" one of their employees to program the game. The deal was struck, and since Howie and I had a prior relationship, I seemed an ideal candidate. The project became a kind of reunion as Howie contracted Jeff Lee to do the artwork.

But I wasn't allowed to work on it while at the office, as it was an outside project and we were being paid as independent contractors for H.A.R. Management, Howie's company. So Williams supplied me with a development cabinet to use at my home, an old FCC sample cabinet from the original *Joust* with a *Bubbles* control panel. (This development cabinet is now in the possession of ACAM, the American Classic Arcade Museum located at the Fun Spot arcade in Weirs Beach, New Hampshire.) After setting it up, I was off and running. Working with Jeff was, as always, a joy. Together we solved the details of how to implement Howie's idea.

Programming the game wasn't difficult, but dispensing tickets became an interesting challenge. To determine how many tickets should be awarded, I had to work out the odds of every possible matching number scenario using combinatorial math, something I'd known pretty well in high school but hadn't used in recent years. After brushing up, I learned some fun mathematical facts about lottery odds. For example, when choosing six numbers out of some larger group, it's more likely to match one or two numbers than it is to match none. So, in *Lotto Fun*, you'd get more tickets for having no matches than for having one or two! That's math.

Other than that, the most challenging aspect of programming the game involved a legal issue that required the presence of a "governor," a software algorithm that ensured the tickets dispensed accurately reflected what the odds said they should be. In a truly random system,

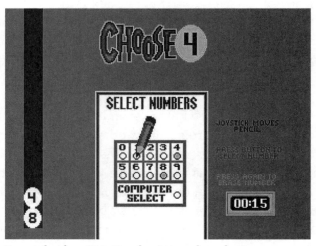

Screen shot from *Lotto Fun* showing number selection.

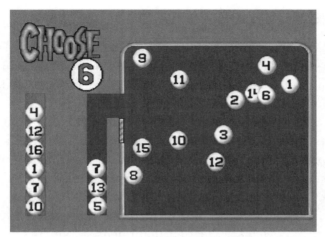

Another *Lotto Fun* screen shot showing balls bouncing randomly around the chamber. There was a simulated suction which would draw a ball into the vertical chamber if it got near the opening.

it's possible for no one to win or for everyone to win. A governor keeps tabs on overall results and basically fudges the results to get things back on track if they're moving too far from statistical norms.

Lotto Fun didn't take very long to program. Once it was done, Betson Enterprises took the circuit boards that Howie had bought from Williams, built the cabinets, and distributed them. I was given one as a gift, but to be honest, it may have been the only game I worked on that I didn't really want to own. But I accepted the gift, and it stayed in my living room in Chicago until I moved to Los Angeles. Then it lived in my garage until the particle-board cabinet literally disintegrated from gradual water damage. All that's left of it right now is the marquee, bezel, electronics, and coin box.

While the physical longevity of that cabinet was short, the longevity of *Lotto Fun* in arcades was surprisingly long. I remember seeing one in an arcade on the New Jersey shore almost fifteen years after its release, just after the new millennium! Crazy.

THE START OF A NEW ERA

Back at my regular day job, I became particularly fascinated with a new product that came out for the Amiga computer: a video digitizer made by a company called A-Squared. Let's unpack all that slowly.

The Amiga was a recently released home computer capable of unprecedented graphics and sound: 4,096 colors! Eight-bit stereo sound! There were image manipulation programs for it that could do things no other computer, including the IBM PC, could do. We had one at Williams not only because of its capabilities, but also because our own Jack Haeger, an immensely talented artist who'd worked on *Sinistar* at Williams a few years earlier, was also the art director for the Amiga design team.

Video digitization is the process of grabbing a video image from some video source, like a camera or a videotape, and converting it into pixel data that a computer system (or video game) could use. A full-color photograph might contain millions of colors, many just subtly different from one another. Even though the Amiga could only display 4,096 colors, that was enough to see an image on its monitor that looked almost perfectly photographic.

Our video game system still could only display 16 colors total. At that level, photographic images were just not possible. But we (and by that I mean everyone working in the video game industry) knew that would change. As memory became cheaper and processors faster, we knew that 256-color systems would soon be possible. In fact, when I started looking into digitized video, our hardware designer, Mark Loffredo, was already playing around with ideas for a new 256-color hardware system.

Let's talk about color resolution for a second. Come on, you know you want to. No worries if you don't, though, you can skip these next few paragraphs if you like. Color resolution is the number of colors a computer system is capable of displaying. And it's all tied in to memory. For example, our video game system could display 16 colors. But artists weren't locked into 16 specific colors. The hardware used a "palette." Artists could choose from a fairly wide range of colors, but only 16 of them could be saved in the palette at any given time. Those colors could be programmed to change while a game was running. In fact, changing colors in a palette dynamically allowed for a common technique used in old video games called "color cycling."

For the hardware to know what color to display at each pixel location, each pixel on the screen had to be identified as one of those 16 colors in the palette. The collection of memory that contained the color values for every pixel on the screen was called "screen memory." Numerically, it takes 4 bits (half a byte) to represent 16 numbers (trust me on the math here), so if 4 bits = 1 pixel, then 1 byte of memory could hold 2 pixels. By contrast, if you wanted to be able to display 256 colors, it would take 8 bits to represent 256 numbers. That's 1 byte (or 8 bits) per pixel.

So you'd need twice as much screen memory to display 256 colors as you would to display 16. Memory wasn't cheap, though, and game manufacturers wanted to keep costs down as much as possible. So memory prices had to drop before management approved doubling the screen memory.

Today we take for granted color resolutions of 24 bits per pixel (which potentially allows up to 16,777,216 colors and true photographic quality). But back then, 256 colors seemed like such a luxury. Even though it didn't approach the 4,096 colors of the Amiga, I was convinced that such a system could result in close to photo-realistic images. And the idea of having movie-quality images in a video game was very exciting to me, so I pitched to management the advantages of getting a head start on this technology. They agreed and bought the digitizer for me to play around with.

The Amiga's digitizer was crude. Very crude. It came with a piece of hardware that plugged into the Amiga on one end, and to the video output of a black-and-white surveillance camera (sold separately) on the other. The camera needed to be mounted on a tripod so it didn't move. You pointed it at something (that also couldn't move), and put a color wheel between the camera and the subject. The color wheel was a circular piece of plastic divided into quarters with different tints: red, green, blue, and clear. When you started the digitizing process, a motor turned the color wheel very slowly, and in about thirty to forty seconds you had a full-color digitized image of your subject. "Full-color" on the Amiga meant 4 bits of red, green, and blue—or 12-bit color, resulting in a total of 4,096 colors possible.

It's hard to believe just how exciting this was! At that time, it was like something from science fiction. And the coolness of it wasn't so much how it worked (because it was pretty damn clunky) but the potential that was there. The Amiga digitizer wasn't practical—the camera and subject needed to be still for so long, and the time it took to grab each image made the process mind-numbingly slow—but just having the ability to produce 12-bit images at all enabled me to start exploring algorithms for color reduction.

Color reduction is the process of taking an image with a lot of colors (say, up to the 16,777,216 possible colors in a 24-bit image) and finding a smaller number of colors (say, 256) to best represent that image. If you could do that, then those 256 colors would form a palette, and every pixel in the image would be represented by a number—an "index" that pointed to one of the colors in that palette. As I mentioned earlier, with a palette of 256 colors, each index could fit into a single byte.

But I needed an algorithm to figure out how to pick the best 256 colors out of the thousands that might be present in a digitized image. Since there was no internet back then, I went to libraries and began combing through academic journals and technical magazines, searching for research done in this area. Eventually, I found some! There were numerous papers written on the subject, each outlining a different approach, some easier to understand than others. Over the next few weeks, I implemented a few of these algorithms for generating 256 color palettes using test images from the Amiga digitizer. Some gave better results than others. Images that were inherently monochromatic looked the best, since many of the 256 colors could be allotted to different shades of a single color.

During this time, Loffredo was busy developing his 256-color hardware. His plan was to support multiple circuit boards, which could be inserted into slots as needed, much like a PC. A single board would give you one surface plane to draw on. A second board gave you two planes, foreground and background, and so on. With enough planes, and by having each plane scroll horizontally at a slightly different rate, you could give the illusion of depth in a side-scrolling game

All was moving along smoothly until the day word came down that Eugene Jarvis had completed his MBA and was returning to Williams to head up the video department. This was big news! I think most people were pretty excited about this. I know I was, because despite our movement toward 256-color hardware, the video department was still without a strong leader at the helm. Eugene, given his already legendary status at Williams, was the perfect person to take the lead, partly because he had some strong ideas of where to take the department, and also due to management's faith in him. Whereas anybody else would have to convince management to go along with an idea, Eugene pretty much had carte blanche in their eyes. Once he was back, he told management what we needed to do and they made sure he, and we, had the resources to do it.

This meant, however, that Loffredo's planar hardware system was toast. Eugene had his own ideas, and everyone quickly jumped on board. He wanted to create a 256-color system based on a new CPU chip from Texas Instruments, the 34010 GSP (Graphics System Processor). The 34010 was revolutionary in that it included graphics-related features within its core. Normally, CPUs would have no direct connection to the graphics portion of the hardware, though there might be some co-processor to handle graphics chores (such as Williams' proprietary VLSI blitter). But the 34010 had that capability on board, obviating the need for a graphics co-processor.

Looking at the 34010's specs, however, revealed that the speed of its graphics functions, while well-suited for light graphics work such as spreadsheets and word processors, was certainly not fast enough for pushing pixels the way we needed. So Mark Loffredo went back to the drawing board to design a VLSI blitter chip for the new system.

Around this time, a new piece of hardware arrived in the marketplace that signaled the next generation of video digitizing. It was called the Image Capture Board (ICB), and it was developed by a group within AT&T called the EPICenter (which eventually split from AT&T and became Truevision). The ICB was one of three boards offered, the others being the VDA (Video Display Adapter, with no digitizing capability) and the Targa (which came in three different configurations: 8-bit, 16-bit, and 24-bit).

The ICB came with a piece of software called TIPS that allowed you to digitize images and do some minor editing on them. All of these boards were designed to plug in to an internal slot on a PC running MS-DOS, the original text-based operating system for the IBM PC. (You may be wondering . . . where was Windows? Windows 1.0 was introduced in 1985, but it was terribly clunky and not widely used or accepted. Windows really didn't achieve any kind of popularity until version 3.0, which arrived in 1990, a few years after the release of Truvision's boards.)

A little bit of trivia: the TGA file format that's still around today (though not as popular as it once was) was created by Truevision for the TARGA series of boards.

The ICB was a huge leap forward from the Amiga digitizer in that you could use a color video camera (no more black-and-white camera or color wheel), and the time to grab a frame was drastically reduced—not quite instantaneous, as I recall, but only a second or two, rather than thirty or forty seconds. And it internally stored colors as 16-bits, rather than 12 like the Amiga. This meant 5 bits each of red, green, and blue—the same that our game hardware used—resulting in a true-color image of up to 32,768 colors, rather than 4,096. Palette reduction would still be a crucial step in the process.

The greatest thing about the Truevision boards was they came with a Software Development Kit (SDK), which meant I could write my own software to control the board, tailoring it to my specific needs. This was truly amazing! Once again, I was so excited about the possibilities that my head was spinning.

I think it's safe to say that most people making video games in those days thought about the future. We realized that the speed and memory limitations we were forced to work under were a temporary constraint. We realized that whether the video game industry was a fad or not, we were at the forefront of a new form of storytelling. Maybe this was a little more true for me because of my interest in filmmaking, or maybe not. But my experiences so far in the game industry fueled my imagination about what might come. And for me, the holy grail was interactive movies. The notion of telling a story in which the player was not a passive viewer but an active participant was extremely compelling. People were already experimenting with it under the constraints of current technology. *Zork* and the rest of Infocom's text adventure games were probably the earliest examples, and more would follow with every improvement in technology. But what I didn't know was if the technology needed to achieve my end goal—fully interactive movies with film-quality graphics—would ever be possible in my lifetime.

I didn't dwell on these visions of the future. They were just thoughts in my head. Yet, while it's nice to dream, at some point you've got to come back down to earth. If you don't take the one step in front of you, you can be sure you'll never reach your ultimate destination, wherever that may be.

I dove into the task and began learning the specific capabilities of the board, as well as its limitations. With the first iteration of my software, which I dubbed WTARG ("W" for Williams, "TARG" for TARGA), you could grab a single image from either a live camera or a videotape. I added a few different palette reduction algorithms so you could try each and find the best palette for that image. More importantly, I added the ability to find the best palette for a group of images, since all the images of an animation needed to have a consistent look. There was no chroma key functionality in those early boards, so artists would have to erase the background manually. I added some tools to help them do that.

This was a far cry from what I ultimately hoped for,

which was a system where we could point a camera at live actors and instantly have an animation of their action running on our game hardware. But it was a start.

SUBURBAN WARFARE

Once we had a working prototype of Eugene and Loffredo's new 34010-based game hardware, we needed some generic software to make it usable. Eugene wrote an operating system, and I wrote a display system. Both could be modified as needed for whatever game was to be written, and served as a starting point to help bootstrap development. With the hardware designed, prototypes built, tools written, and basic software in place, the next step was to start making games!

One of Eugene's mandates was a re-configuration of the offices, so all the people working on video were in the same place. This meant the end of the Dead Zone and a move into a different area of the building. We were still a fairly small group, but we had enough manpower to divide into two teams. Eugene and I were the only programmers, and Jack Haeger and John Newcomer were the only artists. At some point, George Petro was hired as a programmer. George had just graduated from college, so he was pretty green, but he'd also been hanging around Williams since he was a teenager. So Eugene, George, and Jack became one team, and John Newcomer and I became another.

Eugene, Jack, and George started developing the game that would become *NARC*. John and I began working on our own game, a modern take on the classic black-and-white game *Tank*. I'd always been a fan of that game, in which two players looked down at a maze containing two tanks, each controlled by pair of joysticks. The combinations of moving either joystick forward or backward provided maneuvering capability, and a button on top of one of the sticks let you shoot at your opponent.

I was jazzed about doing a tank game with our new digitization capability because I knew we could build models and digitize them to achieve photo-quality realism. John seemed jazzed about that, too, and it wasn't long before he was off to the hobby store, buying some plastic model kits of tanks. John was meticulous in assembling and painting what looked like a perfectly real tank, scaled down to model size, of course. We digitized the turret separately from the base, so the two could move independently.

But what environment would these realistic tanks inhabit? Well, John knew a lot about model kits. He ordered kits of suburban homes as well as businesses like McDonald's and 7-Eleven. Our playfield became a suburban neighborhood, and it wasn't long before we had a premise for the game: the USSR had invaded the United States, leading to a ground war with tanks. What's more, the military had been vanquished, and our last hope was the grassroots efforts of some ass-kicking rebels hell bent on protecting their typically American suburban neighborhood. Remember, this was the 1980s.

As I've mentioned before, I'm not usually one to start naming things up front, but things were done differently at Williams, and John had a lot of experience there. He came up with the name *USSA*, a melding of USSR and USA. And just like that, we had a title!

EXPLODING BODY PARTS

With the leap to 256 colors and our new ability to have near-photographic images in our games, you might

Mark Loffredo, our hardware designer, digitized in *NARC*. This still appeared between levels. The larger image allowed for more detail, although it was still heavily cleaned up by artist Jack Haeger using the usual artists' tools.

wonder if we gave any thought to the implications such a leap might have on our audience (besides noticing how cool it was, I mean). After all, it was one thing for a player to shoot cars, planes, or people when they looked like blocks of pixels or cartoons, but what about when they looked somewhat real? Especially people! This wasn't really an issue on *USSA*, since you never saw humans in our game, just vehicles.

But one day, I heard a lot of laughing and screaming coming from the *NARC* side of the office. Our hardware designer, Mark Loffredo, had been digitized into the game as one of the bad guys. Even though the graphics were crude, he was somewhat recognizable. And the new feature that had just been implemented let the player hit that character with a grenade and explode him into flaming body parts. In all fairness, I have to admit—it was pretty cool. Arms, legs, torso, head, all aflame, rotating and flying in different directions after the impact. It was funny in the way you laugh at a horror movie when something overly gross happens. I grew up on horror movies and had a pretty high tolerance for gore, even though I was never a fan of movies with gore just for the hell of it.

So while I admired that they'd achieved a clear leap in what you could do graphically (after all, it was my digitizing software they were using to get those images), I still questioned the use of this new ability without thinking about its consequences. I said as much to the group as we stood around the monitor, watching the new feature in action. I wasn't scolding or being holier-than-thou. I just asked the question: "Should we be doing this?"

A lively discussion ensued, with most people being on the side of "why not?" I brought up the notion that our games went into arcades, which are often populated with young children. What if they saw these images? What if they played this game? All I wanted was for them to acknowledge the questions. No one seemed to care much, and as the discussion heated up, people gradually walked away. Eventually George was the only one left arguing with me. He vehemently believed in our right (and maybe obligation) to push the envelope, and I continued arguing for taking some responsibility and looking beyond our own satisfaction to consider the bigger picture. Neither side swayed the other, and of course the flaming body parts stayed in the game.

But that argument always stayed with me. My own conscience was clear, as no game that I'd been in charge of had ventured into R-rated territory.

The topic of violence in video games wasn't new. As early as 1982, there were news reports expressing concern about video games promoting violent behavior in children. The addition of graphically violent images would only make the issue more of a concern. But that and further debate was still on the horizon. *NARC*, after all, wasn't even out the door yet. I wound up having more personal connections with this issue later in my career.

I saw George at a retro-gaming event recently and reminded him of our argument so long ago. He didn't remember it, but smiled as he listened, then shrugged and said, "Well, I was young!" It's amazing how your perspectives change once you become a parent.

NARC VS. USSA

I could never have predicted that my time at Williams would end up being so short, especially when things were looking so rosy. The video department was revitalized with Eugene's return and the development of our 256-color system. Our tools were in place, including the ability to digitize images and generate palettes. And we had two teams simultaneously working on new games. Nowhere in my imagination did I think of those teams as being in competition. But I was dead wrong. Even later, when it became obvious there was something going on, I couldn't bring myself to believe that there would actually be a winner and a loser.

From my perspective, development of *USSA* was moving along nicely. John furiously bought and built more model kits, we digitized grass and roads, and then I assembled all these elements into a neighborhood for the tanks to traverse. John also made damaged versions of each building, which would appear in the game when those structures took a hit.

In another departure from the original *Tank* game, and in keeping with the theme of a grassroots rebellion against Russian invaders, John thought that the player should be driving a 4-by-4 pick-up truck. What's more American than that? And in order to make it a fair fight, the player's truck came equipped with a rocket launcher in the back. This led to the bold choice of using a steering wheel and gas pedal as the main controls.

That decision took us down a whole new road (no pun intended). My original thought was to keep all vehicles on the streets, mimicking the maze-like feel of the original *Tank* game. But that seemed too limiting with a steering wheel available, so we relaxed that condition. But what about the rocket launcher? How would a player control that? My idea was a little out there: when a rocket was launched (via a button press), the truck would stop and the steering wheel would guide the rocket until it hit something or flew off-screen. Then the wheel would switch back to steering the truck. It was different from anything I'd ever seen before, and weird though it was, both John and I thought it worked surprisingly well.

Single-player games were going out of vogue at the time. Two or more players meant a game could collect more coins. So *USSA* was designed for two players, with each player able to play independently. They could cooperate or not, but the tanks were always the bad guys. However, this created a problem of scope. In the old *Tank* game, the tanks were small and the maze was confined to a single screen. Our tanks were bigger, and a single screen maze with two players wouldn't allow for much movement. We could make the neighborhood bigger than the screen, but then what would happen if the players drove off in opposite directions? We wouldn't be able to fit them both without scaling the entire world down, and that was something we didn't have the ability to do in this initial version of our hardware.

The only solution that made sense was a split-screen. Each player would always be at the center of their half of the screen, and the neighborhood would scroll as necessary. If they were close to each other, both trucks would be visible on both halves of the screen. If they weren't, no biggie. You could play independently and everything would still work.

Or at least, John and I thought it would. We were very excited about how the game was shaping up. For one thing, it looked fantastic. The digitized graphics gave it a photo-realistic feel you'd never seen in a video game. (LaserDisc games had movie-like graphics, sure, but they weren't interactive in the same way a traditional video game was.) The controls were unique, and it was fun to play! Though not everyone else at Williams agreed.

Steve Ritchie is a legendary pinball designer. Even back then, he was at the top of his game with a string of monster hits. It seemed like he could do no wrong. He and Eugene were very tight, and seemed to share common sensibilities about games. It's no stretch to say they were Williams' golden boys. But despite the fact that Steve's domain was pinball, not video, he had strong opinions about video games, and that included the still-evolving *USSA*. He was not shy about voicing his displeasure with our game.

Somehow, I still didn't believe there was any competition between *NARC* and *USSA*. I envisioned a future where both games rolled off the assembly line. While I fully expected Eugene's game would be first, I didn't see a problem in having *USSA* ready to go when *NARC* wound down. However, upper management, influenced by what they were hearing, felt differently.

Ultimately, *USSA* was canceled. Though I'd been aware of the internal resistance to the game, I still felt blindsided. After all, it wasn't finished yet. It wasn't tuned and it had never been on test, so we never even got any feedback outside of the company. But it was canceled all the same, and that stung more than Frank Ballouz's decision to not take *Us vs. Them* to the AOE show. Because as angry as I was then, I at least knew that development on *Us vs. Them* would continue to completion. All of our efforts on *USSA* had been for nothing. And I'd been so optimistic about its possibilities for success.

I was called into Eugene's office to get the news about *USSA*. Eugene is a genial guy, and my impression was that he wasn't comfortable with certain managerial duties. Such as telling someone their game has been canceled. He's a coder at heart, not a manager, but managing the department was the cost of bringing his vision to Williams. So he had to be the one to break the news, which he did as kindly as was possible. He also mentioned during that meeting that management was keen on doing a football-themed game next, and asked if I was interested in making that my next project. I told him I wasn't. I'd played touch football as a kid, but I knew next to nothing about pro football and cared even less. After explaining this to Eugene, he got a call from Ken Fedesna, our VP of Engineering. Ken wanted me to come down to his office.

Ken was a good guy whom I'd always liked and respected. When I got to his office, he expressed his condolences about *USSA* being canceled and asked if Eugene had told me I'd been assigned to the football game. Time froze for a moment as I processed his question. After realizing the implications, I answered, "No. He asked if I *wanted* to do the football game, but I said no." Ken then let me know as gently as possible that the next game would indeed be a football game, and there was no other project for me to work on. Eugene had tried to soft-sell it to me, but in management's eyes, it was a done deal. I wasn't supposed to say no.

I walked out of that meeting shattered and unsure about what to do next. I felt an urge to just quit then and there, but I know enough about myself not to take drastic actions when I'm angry or upset. I decided to wait it out, take my time, and look for other options. Fortunately, I didn't have to look long because, serendipitously, I got a call within maybe a week or two from Gil Pollack, former VP of Pinball at Gottlieb.

When Gottlieb closed its doors, Gil had bought up a lot of its manufacturing equipment for pinball games, as well as the rights to use the "Gottlieb" name on new pinball machines. He also hired most of Gottlieb's pinball department and started up a new company called Premier Technology. Apparently, making new Gottlieb pinball games had been going well for the last couple of years, and he now thought it might be time to venture into the land of video games. He was looking for someone to lead the effort, someone to build a video game system from scratch and write their first game. I was flattered. I felt up to the challenge, and the timing couldn't have been better.

I gave my notice and left Williams for the first (but as it turned out, not the last) time, on what I hoped were good terms. Despite the way things had gone down, there were no "bad guys" at Williams, or for that matter at any point in my career. I may have disagreed with people. I may have been disappointed by the actions or decisions of others. And I may not have become close friends with everyone I've worked with. But at the end of the day, I consider myself lucky to have known and worked with every one of those people. Some years after the USSA debacle, Steve Ritchie even apologized to me for his behavior. That's an amazing thing for someone of his stature to do. It's kind of impossible not to like that guy.

CHAPTER NINE

THE PREMIER YEARS

Premier Technology was the phoenix that had risen from the ashes of Gottlieb. Gil Pollack had not only bought all of Gottlieb's pinball assembly line equipment, hired the bulk of its pinball designers and technicians, and acquired the rights to emblazon new pinball machines with the Gottlieb name and logo, but in a stroke of nostalgia, he chose to set up shop and produce these new Gottlieb pinball machines at good old 759 Industrial Drive—the original site of Gottlieb's fledgling video department!

Driving there for my first meeting with Gil was like coming home, and not just because of the building itself. I knew many of the employees there (even though I'd never worked with them directly at Gottlieb) with one exception. Craig Bierwaltes, who designed the sound for *Us vs. Them*, had moved over to Premier after Gottlieb closed. I liked and respected all of those guys, and it was great to see them again.

Gil Pollack could be pretty charming when he wanted to be, but he also had a firm control of this new company, and things usually went the way he wanted. In this case, he wanted Premier to enter the coin-op video game market. My job would be to spearhead the development of a new hardware system, write the system software along with the tools for it, and then make a new game, the first in what was hoped to be a long line. At this point in my career, I felt pretty confident in my ability to do all of that, and I couldn't wait to get started.

To accomplish the first part, Premier subcontracted a company called Pixelab, which happened to consist of two former Gottlieb employees, Jun Yum and Kan Yabumoto. Jun had designed Gottlieb's video game hardware, and Kan had created the game *Mad Planets*. They joined together to form Pixelab after Gottlieb folded, and they'd been taking on a variety of consulting work to stay afloat, as well as working on some of their own ideas. I couldn't be more thrilled to be working with them. I enjoyed the company of these two, and knew they were more than capable of accomplishing the task at hand. We were going to make a great team.

Our headquarters was Pixelab's office in the western suburbs of Chicago. Just as Gottlieb's video operation started in Bensenville, away from its main plant in Northlake, it seemed appropriate to set up Premier's video division in a location away from its main plant in Bensenville. To his credit, Gil was fine with us working on our own. All I asked was that he take advantage of the fact that no one knew Premier was starting a video division, and keep it secret until we had something to announce. That way, we could take the time to get it right and go public with a bang. Gil seemed to agree, and we were off and running.

Naturally, we would need an artist to create any video graphics we required. Luckily, my favorite collaborator, Jeff Lee, was available and joined the team, working mostly out of his home. Jeff's input was valuable in the earliest planning stages, and his role became key once we began working on an actual game.

The first step was designing the hardware. What would be the specs of this new system? How much memory? Which processor? There were a few things I knew I wanted. Video digitization was the future of gaming to me, so I wanted 256-color capability. And I was now familiar with the Texas Instruments 34010 GSP, so I advocated using that as our CPU. Rather than develop a proprietary VLSI chip for high-speed pixel transfer, Jun was in favor of a two-planar system, meaning a foreground and background plane (each capable of 256 colors and each having its own GSP), rather than a single-plane system like Williams used. As with Gottlieb's old hardware, the background plane would be pretty much static, and we would only need to blit sprites in the foreground plane. ("Blitting," in case you've forgotten, just means the transfer of pixels to the screen.) Jun, Kan, and I agreed on all the aspects of the design, and Jun began developing the hardware.

Meanwhile, Kan and I set about designing and coding software tools for the new system. Although Texas Instruments supplied a debugger for its 34010 processor, Kan wanted something a little more robust, so he wrote his own from the ground up and, with a bit of intended whimsy, called it GSPOT.

RETURN OF THE HANDS

It would be a few months before there was a working prototype of our hardware that could be used for actual game development. Since we hadn't yet settled on a game concept, and Premier naturally had final approval on that, there would have to be the inevitable pitch meeting.

I can't remember all the concepts I pitched—I think there were three or four, and I'm guessing the list was similar to the games I'd pitched to Gottlieb in the months before they folded. But the one that Gil and his team seemed the most interested in, to my surprise, was the old "hand squishing flies" concept that I'd coded back at Gottlieb just for our own amusement. The gameplay was so fun and satisfying, and I believed the core concept was sound, but I knew it had to be fleshed out. After some reflection, I started to think that with video digitizing and 256 colors, we could make a much better, more photo-realistic pair of hands.

I've recently found some YouTube videos reviewing this game (which came to be known as *Exterminator*). Inevitably, the reviewers express some version of "What were these guys smoking when they came up with this?" I can state quite firmly that the genesis of the concept involved no illicit hallucinogens. That's not to say it didn't fly off the rails somewhere along the way—it did—but drugs weren't involved.

The early stages of development went smoothly. And why not? We were working under no deadline or pressure. The first prototype of the hardware was a single-layer circuit board with a lot of wire-wrapped components, but it was sufficient for running our tools and system software until the final mass-produced circuit boards became available. One problem that plagued us early on was noise. Sometimes the hardware reset itself in the middle of running some test program. Not good, but Jun felt that the final production boards wouldn't have that problem.

Once the prototype hardware was available, it was time to flesh out the design. The original game was just about squishing flies in your hand. That was tons of fun for a bunch of guys taking a break from work for a few minutes, but it didn't seem enough for a game that would sit in an arcade and collect quarters. Jeff once again became my sounding board, although his working at a distance made that more difficult.

I thought about what you could do with your hand besides make a fist. Well, you could pound that fist on the ground. This opened up the idea of having not only flying insects but crawling ones. And I needed an enemy. (The original Gottlieb version had none.) A wasp seemed like a perfect insect enemy. And how would you get rid of a pesky wasp? By shaking your hand! What else could you do with your hand? Well, you could point your finger and pretend to shoot. And since this was a video game, you didn't have to pretend. I'd program it so you could actually shoot with your "finger." This idea of shooting required me to add depth to the game—the original had taken place on a flat plane with no background. But the idea of adding depth meant the player was killing bugs within some space—say, a room—which led naturally to the notion of the player being an Exterminator.

The basic structure of the game was straightforward. The player (a disembodied hand) was the Exterminator, traveling from house to house on a street with a cul-de-sac. The player needed to clear each room in the house, which would contain a variety of enemies. I didn't want to repeat the tuning problem of Q*bert, where the game's difficulty stays the same after Level 5. Instead, I wanted the difficulty to ramp up sufficiently, so the game became challenging without being off-putting. I retained the two-player setup of the original, with one player controlling a right hand and the other, the left hand. As previously mentioned, two-player games had become pretty standard in the coin-op industry.

Jeff and I agreed that the look of the bugs should be a little on the cartoony side since the whole concept was somewhat surreal (not unlike Q*bert). I was also cognizant of people's natural aversion to insects, so I didn't want the graphics to be too realistic and gross people out. This played into the decision to create some non-insect enemies. As always, Jeff's input was welcome and indispensable. I have absolutely no idea which of us thought up which enemies. I just knew I wanted there to be a lot of variety so I'd have lots of elements to play with and combine as the game progressed.

When it came time to start programming the game, I had an office built in my basement at home and set up a development system there. I was able to digitize my own hand as the player's hand. Jeff was coming up with amazing digitized art for the enemies and background. Much as John Newcomer had built models to digitize for the unreleased *USSA*, Jeff built models to create the cul-de-sac and van for the screen showing the Exterminator moving from house to house. He also digitized parts of his own home to make the playfields.

We truly let our imaginations run wild. Maybe too much so, given that many reactions to the game involved the belief that either drugs or insanity were involved in its creation. And there may have been a small nugget of truth in the insanity part, as my marriage was becoming strained at the time due to factors that had nothing to do with video games. In the middle of the development of *Exterminator*, I separated from my wife.

It was a trial separation, and during that time I rented an apartment just a few blocks' walking distance from my house. I moved my development system with me, and the bulk of the development of this game took place there. I would make trips to Pixelab occasionally, or to see Jeff or meet with Premier once in a while. But most of the time I was coding away in isolation, in what my kids were told was my "office." The separation lasted about nine months. During that time, my wife and I went to counseling, where I'm happy to say we were able to resolve things. I eventually moved back home.

I don't necessarily look at the separation as a dark time in my life, although there were certainly difficult days and my ability to think creatively was affected on some level. Overall, I'm grateful for it, because without it I'm fairly certain the marriage would have ended then and there. But trying to come up with a satisfying game design over those months was challenging.

As if that weren't enough of a strain, the development of *Exterminator* was plagued with other problems. For one thing, shortly after we started the project, Gil Pollack was interviewed in a trade magazine and, despite our agreement that we would keep things quiet for now, he announced proudly that Premier was starting a video game division. He even gave a release date for *Exterminator*, saying it would debut at the 1989 ACME (American Coin Machine Expo) trade show in Las Vegas. The fact that we had never even committed to that date internally didn't seem to matter to him. I'm not one for hype, but the same can't be said for Gil, who had hyped up our debut as the second coming of video games. This added a pressure we did not need, and reduced time for solving problems that arose.

And arise they did! Although I thought programming the hand to do all these things (squishing, pounding, shooting, shaking) was very cool, there wasn't a joystick in existence that could do everything we needed it to. Obviously we needed basic joystick movement to move the hand around the plane of the screen, and a thumb button to make a fist. But we also wanted the hand to shoot, so we needed a trigger button as well. So far, so good. An off-the shelf joystick could do all that. But to aim your shots, we needed the ability to rotate the on-screen hand, which meant the joystick itself needed to rotate and then report its rotation via a device called a potentiometer. No such joystick existed.

Luckily, Premier had a relationship with a company called Happ Controls, which supplied a lot of video game and pinball parts. I contacted an engineer there who believed he could work up a solution to our problem. Gil was on board with the extra cost, so they went ahead and made a prototype.

Meanwhile, the final circuit boards started coming in and Jun put together some development cabinets. Unfortunately, the noise problems from the prototypes did not go away and whenever the game ran, it would randomly freeze. Jun tried to fix it by wiring in other components to alleviate the noise, but nothing seemed to help. I had to put in special software, which responded to an early detection of the problem by putting up a screen of information (somewhat similar to the Windows Blue Screen of Death), but the system would be hosed after that point and have to be reset.

Still, as Jun frantically tried to solve the noise issues, game development continued and eventually *Exterminator* was ready to be put on test in arcades. Watching people play, I could see that they were having a hard time learning to control their virtual hand. Initially, I allowed the player to shoot at any time, and if I remember correctly, moving the joystick up and down moved your hand deeper into the room and back. Buttons on the control panel moved the hand up and down. Clearly, I needed to make some changes to simplify the controls. I eventually settled on a scheme where you could only shoot when you positioned your hand at the far edge of the screen (meaning the left edge for the "left-handed" player and the right edge for the "right-handed" player). From there, you could rotate or move up and down so your shots could reach any part of the room. It was a compromise, but I felt that once a player understood how it worked, they'd master it. If the game didn't freeze on them, that is.

Of course, once you put a game in an arcade and people don't like it, it's unlikely that they'll try a new version of it. That's why after a re-design, you'd normally put the game on test in a different arcade. I have a vague memory that after a substantial re-tooling of *Exterminator*, we may have put it back in the same arcade a couple of weeks later with a sign attached that proclaimed: "New Version!"

The joystick developed by Happ Controls went through a few iterations of design before achieving playability, but it finally got there. Or so we thought. Once the game was out on test, we found the controller breaking frequently. Wires inside the control panel would just snap. It took us a while to figure out that in adding the ability to rotate the joystick, Happ didn't include a way to limit that rotation. Little kids would just rotate and rotate the stick until the wires inside became taut and snapped. Once we understood the problem, Happ engineered a solution, but it took more time—time we didn't really have.

There was a term coming into use around then for software that was promised but never materialized: "vaporware." I didn't want *Exterminator* to be perceived that way. I knew I had to bust my ass to get this game working. But I couldn't do anything about the noise problems or the joystick. And without getting valid test data from location testing, I couldn't adequately tune the game.

VEGAS, BABY!

All of these pressures accumulated as the weeks leading up to the ACME show in Vegas melted away. Jun finally admitted that using a single-layer circuit board was a major factor in the noise problems and set about designing a double-layer board to replace it, but we wouldn't have that in time for Vegas. And because of all the various problems, our coin collection numbers (the number of quarters collected by the game while out on test) were terrible. So Gil really had nothing on paper to show off to the distributors at ACME.

With everything else on my plate, I never got involved with the cabinet design for the game. That was honestly the least of my worries . . . until Gil called me in to Premier's offices to show me the cabinet they'd come up with. It was bright orange and looked like a house! I was a little shocked. I wasn't expecting anything revolutionary or even different, but this was . . . definitely different! It made a statement, but I don't think the statement was "Man, I really want to play this game!" Regardless, that was our cabinet. No protesting on my part was going to change it, and there was no time to change it, anyway.

At the last minute, Gil made the wise choice not to put a row of playable *Exterminator* cabinets on the show floor. Instead, as was sort of common with games that were "not quite ready," he had a couple of them set up in a private suite for only a few of the biggest or most important distributors to see under controlled conditions.

My memories of being in Las Vegas for that show are vague, which isn't surprising as I'm sure I got very little sleep leading up to it. I do remember that, as a tease, Gil set up an *Exterminator* cabinet on the main show floor in a partially opened cardboard box, so only the very top of the cabinet was visible. Leaning on a hand-truck, the barely visible, mostly boxed cabinet sported a sign saying *"The Exterminator* . . . Coming Early Oct. '89." Great showmanship, that Gil. I have to give him that.

We showed the game to various people privately in the suite, always crossing our fingers that it wouldn't freeze up. When it did, we explained that the double-layered boards were coming and would solve the problem. In truth, we could only hope they would.

After the show, the game received some industry press that mostly praised its originality and innovation, its riskiness at being so "different," and its graphics. (Very few games at the time had embraced digitizing to the extent that we had. Even the games that Williams

A puff piece about *Exterminator* in the October 1989 issue of *Replay*, one of the coin-op industry's trade magazines.

made using my digitizing system after I left—*NARC*, *Trog*, *Hi-Impact Football*—didn't seem quite so photo-realistic.) Still, without decent coin data to prove that the game could collect, and with word-of-mouth stories about the freezes and joystick problems, orders did not rush in. Even though the double-sided boards did fix

A somewhat mixed review from *Advanced Computer Entertainment* magazine, January 1990.

the noise problems and Happ's engineers were able to limit the joystick's rotation so that the wires underneath wouldn't snap, only about 250 *Exterminators* were built. And though some of the factors that led to its failure were out of my control, I've always felt responsible. Because even if everything else had gone perfectly, I don't know that it ever would have found mainstream acceptance. It's just an oddball of a game.

I had an opportunity to play it recently, after not seeing a playable cabinet for at least twenty years. I was surprised at how much I enjoyed it. I reclaimed a small bit of pride toward the game that day.

As a side note, I should mention that Premier hired a company called Audiogenic to make home versions of *Exterminator* for a multitude of platforms. I don't remember being involved in that at all, but I can't blame Gil for trying to recoup some of his losses. I have no idea how well that game sold or how much money Premier Technology earned from it, but if you surf the internet you'll find more pages about the home versions than the arcade version.

MOVING ON

To say that Gil was disappointed in the performance of *Exterminator* is a bit of an understatement. My relationship with Premier became somewhat strained. But a video game system is more than just the first game you create on it. We (finally) had a stable circuit board, all the system development tools, art tools . . . everything you need to create a game. Just because *Exterminator* failed didn't mean the next game wouldn't. *Reactor* wasn't the hit that Gottlieb expected, and *Pro-Vid-Guard-Argus* never even made it out the door. It wasn't until *Q*bert* that

Gottlieb had a hit. I fully expected Premier to get started on another game as soon as possible. I just wasn't sure if I would be the one to create it.

It was after a couple of weeks of silence that I finally got the call: "Let's have another pitch meeting for a second game." I was ready for it. I had become very interested in doing a side-scrolling, character-based game, much in the visual style of the recent *Teenage Mutant Ninja Turtles* arcade game that had just been released. The characters were cartoonish, but large. Our 256-color system would be ideally suited to making such characters look as good as they would on a television. My game was to be called *Lab Rat*, and the player character was a human-sized rabbit that had been the subject of genetic experiments and given human qualities. (I'm not sure what it is with me and rabbits—remember *Bunny Bondage*?) And yes, I'm aware that the game was to be named *Lab RAT*, not *Lab Rabbit*. My thinking was that the character was *treated* like a lab rat.

Anyway, the premise of the game was that the player was a genetically enhanced rabbit trapped in a sub-sub-sub-basement of some government facility. To escape, it would have to ascend through all of the floors above it. You'd be able to see parts of two floors at a time, one above the other. Since each floor would be much wider than the width of the monitor, you'd have to move through your current floor until you could find a stairway or elevator, or some means of moving up to the next higher floor. Of course, along the way you'd have to fight a variety of enemies using whatever skills were at your disposal, or whichever skills you'd discovered along the way.

I was pretty excited about this concept, and pitched it with my usual degree of enthusiasm. Then, once again, I just waited for a phone call. Eventually that call came, and the news was not good. Premier had decided not to use me to create their second game. I was disappointed, but not crushed. After all, I'd known it was a possibility. I wished them well and offered to help if any roadblocks came up along the way.

The question arose . . . who would they get to create their next game? As it turns out, a few months earlier they'd hired a young new programmer whom I'd sort of taken under my wing. I brought him up to speed on the hardware and software tools, and he would have been something of an apprentice to me if I'd worked on the next game. What I found out some time later was that he'd convinced Gil that he could program a game of his own design in a fraction of the time (and cost) that I'd proposed for *Lab Rat*. The fact that he'd never made a game before didn't seem to dissuade Gil at all. Maybe Gil's thinking was that I'd never programmed a game before *Q*bert*, and I did okay. Why not give this kid a try? Of course, I did have a master's degree and some programming experience before *Q*bert*, plus an apprenticeship of sorts working on *Pro-Vid-Guard-Argus*. At any rate, I was out and he was in.

I'd periodically get reports from my friends inside Premier about his progress, and apparently that project did not go well. He was in way over his head from the beginning and the game was never completed or released. Premier's foray into video games was over and I was sad about that, because the potential for that system was huge. But unlike Gottlieb, which went in big—hiring an entire division to make video games—Premier reacted to the failure of *Exterminator* by putting all the pressure for success on the shoulders of an inexperienced newbie.

So after two years working with Premier, I found myself out of a job. But not for long. As seemed to happen many times in my life, another opportunity came along at just the right time. Surprisingly, it came from my old

Gottlieb colleagues, Jun Yum and Kan Yabumoto, better known as Pixelab. Though they both spoke English very well, it was their second language (they were Korean and Japanese, respectively), and they liked the idea of having me, an American, as part of their company. Since we worked really well together, they offered to keep me on part-time, to serve three roles. The first was technical, helping them with whatever projects they had going. Second, as a native English speaker, I was well-suited to writing technical documentation for any products they developed. In fact, Kan's GSPOT debugger had become so useful, they had decided to release it to the general public. I ended up writing the manual.

The other role? To be their token American—going to client meetings and mostly just sitting there, being "not Asian." I didn't mind this at all. Personally, I found it hard to believe anyone would discriminate against them for being Asian, but it was a concern of theirs that it might happen. And if my presence actually dissuaded anyone from discriminating against them, well, that was all right by me.

Working part-time was convenient for me, as acting had become a more significant part of my life over the past couple of years. While I'd been doing plays in small theaters for a long while (always on nights or weekends), the flexibility of my work schedule on *Exterminator* had allowed me to go to auditions and take on acting jobs I wouldn't have been able to do if I'd worked a traditional 9-to-5 job. Mostly these were industrial films or low-budget commercials, and I also got to be an understudy in some of Chicago's biggest productions. In 1991, during my time with Pixelab, I booked a small role in the Goodman Theatre's production of *The Visit* by Friedrich Durrenmatt. The role consisted primarily of me (with the help of another actor) carrying the lead actress, Rosalind

Cash, around on a sedan chair and playing music on a melodica. Since the role had no dialogue, I auditioned by playing the piano. After I was hired, the Goodman supplied a melodica for me to use, even though I happened to own one. It had been given to me by my grandmother. She'd won it when she was once an audience member of Steve Allen's talk show. But I digress.

My experience working at the Goodman was amazing. Everything there was top-notch. The set cost an ungodly amount. My costume, which consisted of a luxuriously tailored Italian suit, overcoat, and shoes, was worth more than my salary over the entire run of the show. And I got to work with some of Chicago's finest actors, as well as the leads who were brought in from out of town. I mentioned Rosalind Cash, whose geek cred for me was that she was in *The Omega Man* playing opposite Charlton Heston. The male lead was Josef Sommer, an accomplished actor who'd appeared in many movies, but for me, the most notable was *Close Encounters of the Third Kind*. Just being around these actors was thrilling. I helped Rosalind learn her lines, and shared some meals with Josef and other cast members. I shared a dressing room with three guys, one of whom was Steve Pink, who would eventually direct *Hot Tub Time Machine*.

Despite having no lines to say or any real acting to do, this experience gave me the ability to think of myself as an actor without snickering. Apart from Steppenwolf Theatre, the Goodman was pretty much the pinnacle of Chicago theater. For the first time, I began to envision the possibility of an acting career in my future. Perhaps the video game industry had run its course for me. I was still a bit stung from the failure of *Exterminator*. There was a time when I'd thought I could spend my entire life making games. That seemed less and less likely now.

And then . . . once again . . . I got a phone call.

CHAPTER TEN

RETURN TO WILLIAMS

The unexpected phone call I received in 1991 was from Ken Fedesna, VP of Engineering at Williams, which had become Williams/Bally/Midway just after I'd left in 1988. Bally, one of the original pinball manufacturers, had grown quite a bit in the 1970s and '80s, acquiring casinos, amusement parks, and a chain of health clubs. They also started up a reasonably successful video game division, as did most other pinball companies around that time. But at some point, their grasp exceeded their reach and they needed to sell off part of their empire. Williams bought up the pinball and video game divisions (which included the Midway name after Bally bought the company in 1969) and officially became Williams/Bally/Midway. I'll keep calling them Williams, since it essentially stayed the same company regardless of which name went on a marquee.

The phone call was unexpected because I'd left Williams three years earlier, with some regret over the cancellation of *USSA* and my subsequent reassignment to a game I had no desire to work on. And even though I felt I'd left without burning any bridges, I wasn't sure the folks at Williams felt the same way. It was a huge relief to find out that they did.

So here I was, on the phone with Ken, who explained that they were right in the middle of a major project and one of the programmers had unexpectedly given notice. This game was a licensed project based on what was going to be a very high-profile movie, and they were already behind schedule. They needed someone who could hit the ground running. My familiarity with their system made me an ideal candidate.

Ken's offer made me realize something. Every time I'd left the video game industry, I'd tried to convince myself that I was fine with it. But in truth, I was always itching to get back in, and this was no exception. As it turned out, the property being developed into an arcade game was *Terminator 2: Judgment Day*, the sequel to James Cameron's runaway hit from 1984, *The Terminator*, starring Arnold Schwarzenegger.

Here's a recap, in case you've been living under a rock the past few decades. A company called Cyberdyne creates Skynet, an AI that causes the apocalypse and wipes out most of humanity. The survivors rally together under a man named John Connor. After failing to wipe out the resistance and fearing humanity might eventually win back the planet, Skynet uses a time machine to send a cyborg "Terminator" assassin back in time to kill Connor's mother, Sarah, before the hero can be born.

I was a huge fan of *The Terminator*, and had no idea a sequel was even being made! This was incredible! I couldn't believe my luck. Naturally, I happily accepted the offer and found myself back at California and Roscoe, working for Williams again. In the time since my last stint there, I'd moved from Chicago's Lincoln Park neighborhood to Roscoe Village, which conveniently put me about a mile from the Williams offices. Bicycling to work was a piece of cake, weather permitting.

I was amazed at how much had changed since I'd left Williams three years prior. For one thing, the video department had grown considerably. *NARC* had indeed

Creating Q*bert

been followed by a football game, *High Impact Football*, programmed by a new hire named Ed Boon, later to become the co-creator of *Mortal Kombat*. Then came *Trog*, *Super High Impact*, *Hit the Ice*, and *Total Carnage*. All of this resulted in the video department now working in a much larger and better space than the Dead Zone. It was essentially one massive windowless room, but its interior open space had plenty of room for cubicles, with private offices lining the edge. This time, I was lucky enough to get an actual office!

When I'd left, the video department essentially consisted of Eugene Jarvis, George Petro, Jack Haeger, and John Newcomer. They were all still there, but now there was also the aforementioned Ed Boon, Mark Turmell, John Tobias, Sal Divita, John Carlton, John Vogel, Tony Goskie, and more. There were enough people for multiple teams to be working on a variety of games at the same time. A project might also bring in people from other teams and departments for help, depending on what was needed. And Eugene Jarvis had formed a team to work on his new pet project, a 3D polygon-based system. I'm referring here to a system displaying objects made up of polygons in a 3-dimensional space, rather than a left eye/right eye stereographic 3D system. This was a first for Williams. Arcade hardware wasn't known for being fast enough to pull this off, so Eugene and his team had their work cut out for them, and they spent their time largely apart from the rest of the video department.

George Petro and Jack Haeger, who both worked with Eugene on *NARC*, teamed up afterward to develop *Trog*, a dinosaur maze game that used WTARG to digitize clay images (the video game version of Claymation). I remember seeing it in an arcade and thinking that was a brilliant use for digitizing—one that hadn't occurred to me. With *Trog* behind them, the two were now the *T2* game leads. George was lead programmer and Jack was lead artist. The core team included artists John Vogel and Tim Coman, and two programmers: Bill Dabelstein, a junior programmer nicknamed "Dozer," and Todd Allen, the guy I was replacing. Chris Granner did the music and sounds.

The overall plan for the *T2* game was to follow the story of the film *T2: Judgment Day*. As you probably know, the sequel takes place years after the first film, when John Connor (played by Edward Furlong) is an adolescent and targeted by a more advanced time-traveling assassin, the "liquid metal" T-100 prototype terminator played by Robert Patrick. This time around, John is protected by a reprogrammed Arnold-model Terminator, as well as his hardened, battle-ready mother Sarah (played again by Linda Hamilton).

The story was kept completely secret while the film was being developed; very few people got to see a script. I'm not even sure we had a copy in-house. But George and Jack had gotten to read it and formulated a game design based on what they read. The original script showed more of the future, all the way up to the rebels defeating Skynet and finding its time machine. So the game was divided into two parts: the future (up through the rebels finding the time machine) and the present (after the Terminators have been sent back).

Todd Allen had coded the display system for *T2*, a multi-planar, side-scrolling display system. The illusion of depth was created by making images that were supposed to be in the distance look smaller and scroll slower than the larger, faster scrolling images, which appeared to be up close.

When I joined the *T2* team in June of 1991, much of the "future" section of the game had already been coded. I was asked to program a couple of enemies. One was a floating orb. For this, I recreated the AI of one of the enemies in *Us vs. Them*. The orb knew if a player was aiming at it by detecting the player's targeting cursor, and moved to another quadrant of the screen to avoid getting hit. I added a certain amount of lag to its response, so it wasn't impossible to kill. Another enemy I coded was a snake-like machine made up of linked parts. It slithered toward you from a distance and leaped up to attack when it got close. You could destroy pieces of it anywhere on its body, but only destroying the head would stop its attack.

The images we used were digitized, but I was genuinely stunned to learn that in my three-year absence, nothing had been done with WTARG! I figured someone would take up the mantle and continue to develop that software, taking advantage of cheaper memory and speed improvements to streamline the process. The Targa boards had advanced in those years as well, coming down in price and adding features like chroma key, which would filter out a blue background automatically and make stripping images much less time-consuming.

But no. No one had done any of that. Artists were still

The Targa+ board pictured above was incorporated into our digitizing system after the release of *T2*. In addition to being faster at grabbing frames, it added a crucial ability—chromakey.

videotaping and then playing back the tape, freeze-framing to grab single frames, and hand-stripping out the background. Crazy! I could see exactly how to make the process so much easier, even if the artists using it could not, so I asked for and got approval to purchase some newer Targa boards and began improving WTARG in my spare time.

Many of the images used for the *T2* game came from the film's actual sets. Jack Haeger went to California and took copious amounts of videotape of endoskeletons, miniature models of ships and future enemies, props, and set pieces. For anything he might have missed, we were allowed to use the crew documenting the "making of" the film to shoot video for us. The degree of access was unbelievable. It all came down to James Cameron's excitement about the digitization technology we had. When George and Jack flew to California to pitch him on letting Williams do the arcade game for *T2*, they brought VHS tapes of *NARC*, showing both behind the scenes footage of our process and the results. Cameron was hooked, and granted them all the access they needed.

We even had access to some of the actual actors from the film. Eddie Furlong and Robert Patrick were both videotaped performing actions specifically for our game. We also used Linda Hamilton's stunt double, and Arnold's stunt double, wearing an Arnold mask! All of this was done before I came on board.

At some point, we were sent a rough cut of the movie. It showed the original ending, in which we see a future where Skynet never happened; Sarah Connor is an old woman, and John Connor is a senator in Washington. This was later changed to a more ambiguous ending for the theatrical release, but what a bizarre treat to have seen that original ending years before it eventually made its way onto one of the DVD editions of the film.

Although it was originally hoped that the game would be released around the same time as the movie, that dream evaporated pretty quickly as months rolled by and things still weren't ready. On the other hand, having an early copy of the movie meant I could incorporate digitized video from the film. This presented a challenge because we still had memory, speed, and palette limitations in our hardware that prevented us from doing anything approaching full motion video. But with a judicious amount of number crunching and some cleverness, I was able to put bits of the movie into the game. I used small video windows, a lower-than-ideal frame rate, and compression algorithms to display three short clips when the game transitioned from "future" to "present." I also managed to show a series of short clips at the very end of the game, taken from the end of the film when the T-1000 gets melted (sorry for the belated spoiler alert).

My other contribution to the game was coding the SWAT van level. Much like the scene in the movie, the player escapes from the Cyberdyne office building in a SWAT van while a helicopter flown by the T-1000 tries to crash into it and blow it up. Although this appeared in the original game design in some form, it was going to be scrapped. But I felt it was important as a narrative connection between the Cyberdyne level and the Steel Mill level (where the film's climactic battle takes place), and I had an idea for how to make it work without adding weeks to the schedule. To George and Jack's credit, they let me run with it.

I've always been a fan of adding strategy to a video game rather than just reflex, and to me there was an opportunity here to break up the "shoot everything" style of the game with something different. The helicopter is off-screen and you don't know exactly when it's going to fly into view or from which direction. It takes many hits to destroy, but shooting it also slows it down, and that's what you really want. If it hits the van at full force, the van (meaning the player) blows up. But slow it down, and it may retreat before hitting you. Once the player destroys the helicopter, the T-1000 finds its way into a tanker truck and tries to ram the van from behind (again, just like in the movie). The best strategy for dealing with the truck was basically the same as for the helicopter—shoot it to slow it down and avoid, or at least lessen, the impact from a crash. The tension came from not knowing exactly when the truck would rush in from off-screen.

When our *T2* game was finally released, it was as much of a runaway hit as the movie. One of the most bizarre things to happen in the aftermath of the game was a visit from *Entertainment Tonight*. We were all pretty excited and flattered that we'd be getting some press from what we assumed was to be a puff piece. An *ET* crew came to our offices to interview Jack and George. But as it turned out, this was anything but a puff piece. *ET* was doing a hard-hitting story about violence in video games and making an example of *T2*, which, they claimed, encouraged kids to shoot cops!

They were referring, of course, to the Cyberdyne level of the game where the player (who represents Arnold's Terminator, a *good* guy) is attacked by all manner of SWAT officers (who are just doing their job and think that this big guy in sunglasses carrying weapons is a killer and terrorist). However, in the movie, John Connor has instructed the Terminator not to kill anyone. The Terminator obliges, making sure only to stun, wound, and disarm the cops and SWAT guys. So our game followed that example. The player only shoots to wound people (always in the knee, I might add), not kill. The animation depicting this wasn't graphic or bloody. When shot by the player, a cop would grab his knee, fall down, and then just disappear.

There was also the matter of the T-1000 (the story's main antagonist), which is made of a polymimetic alloy that could assume any shape and texture but spends most of the movie and all of the game in the form of a police officer, and your goal is to destroy him. So the insinuation from the *ET* story was that our game was telling kids to shoot cops.

I couldn't believe this! We were just following the movie! We were duty-bound to adapt it faithfully into a game. That was our goal. Still, I understood there was a valid reason for concern: the movie was rated R, but the game was readily available in many kid-friendly locations. Young kids who hadn't seen the movie might play the game and not totally understand the distinction between a human cop and a shape-shifting machine pretending to be a cop. I thought back to *NARC* and its exploding body parts. The question of how violence or graphic images should be used in video games was a valid one, and still is today. But I also believe context is important, and in the context of this particular story, I thought the *ET* attack was misguided. It's a bit like people who condemn a movie without ever seeing it, just because they don't like the way it sounds.

I thought Jack handled himself particularly well when interviewed. He brought up the fact that his wife was in law enforcement, and he would never promote any game implying that violence against officers was okay. And in the story we were telling—the same as the movie's story—the police weren't bad guys, just obstacles in the good Terminator's way. No moral lesson was being taught here. It was just fantasy. The controversy (if there ever really was one) died down pretty quickly. *ET* filled some airtime, and *T2* went on being a popular game.

While *T2* was in development, other teams were

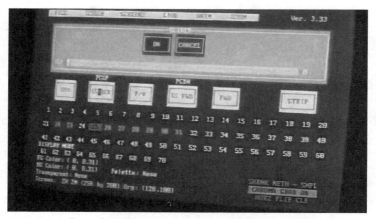

A rare view of one of WTARG's control screens, which among other things, allowed a user to turn individual frames on and off while an animation was running to see how the sequence would look with fewer frames. WTARG ran under MS-DOS, a text-based operating system. I converted it into a Windows program after *Revolution X* was done.

working on their own games. One of these teams consisted of programmer Ed Boon and artist John Tobias. They were creating a new fighting game using digitized images for the characters. When I saw what they were doing, I was blown away. Their human characters were larger than any digitized characters that had come before, and the increased size allowed for more detail. Between *T2* and this new fighting game (which would become *Mortal Kombat*), I really felt like WTARG had come into its own, and was being used the way I had always hoped it would be.

Fun story: One day, Ed Boon came into my office and asked for a favor. He had a full-screen digitized image of the monstrous Goro character, and wanted to use it in *Mortal Kombat*'s "attract mode." The attract mode is the part of a video arcade game that cycles repeatedly when no one is playing. Its goal is to entice (or "attract") a player to pop a quarter into the machine. Well, Ed couldn't afford to store a full-screen image in memory uncompressed—it would leave him little room for the rest of the game—so he wondered if I could compress it down to a usable size. I said, "Sure." Then I added jokingly, "But you'll have to pay me a quarter for every game you sell."

We both laughed and I set to work. As promised, I delivered the compressed data and some decompression code he could run to get the image displayed on the screen. No biggie, I thought, and went on with my own work.

Months later, after *Mortal Kombat* had been rolling off the production line for some time, I found an envelope sitting on my desk. It contained a substantial, if not life-changing, bonus check for my work on that game. This was truly a kind and unexpected gesture. To this day, I'm not sure if that joking conversation with Ed had anything to do with my getting that check or not.

After *T2* was done, I had some free time to go back and work on WTARG, which I happily did. At long last, I added chroma key support so there would be no more tedious hand-stripping out of backgrounds. To take full advantage of this, we would need a space designed for image acquisition. So Jack Haeger took the lead in the creation of our in-house blue screen studio. He purchased some high-end video cameras and professional-quality studio lights, and set about terraforming an unused area in the back of the plant. We already had a treadmill and an assortment of cushioned workout mats for stunts that had been used for a number of games since *NARC*. The treadmill had to have its hand grip removed, which made it more dangerous but usable for our purpose. Because our system was inherently two-dimensional, we needed actors to perform actions at different rotational angles. The more angles we shot, the smoother we could make a digital character's turning motion. So we mapped out lines on the floor and turned the treadmill to face different directions and capture actions at each angle. For forward-facing directions, to prevent obscuring part of the image we were capturing, the handgrip had to go.

Our hardware designer, Mark Loffredo, wasn't resting on his laurels during this period of increased development activity. Our original 256-color system supported only one palette that had to be shared by every on-screen element—characters, backgrounds, everything that appeared at the same time. This could result in some blotchiness, as there were only 256 colors to go around. But lower chip prices allowed Mark to add more memory to our hardware and support up to 16 possible palettes.

Here's how that worked, for those of you who are technically minded. The rest of you are free to skip over the next paragraph. I won't judge.

With 256 possible colors, every pixel on the screen is represented by exactly 1 byte. All of these bytes together are called "screen memory." A byte (which is 8 bits) can represent any number between 0 and 255. So if a color palette consists of 256 colors, each pixel (byte) in screen memory points to a specific color in that 256 color palette. Now imagine that there's another chunk of memory exactly half the size of screen memory. Let's call it "palette memory." In this chunk, for every pixel on the screen, there's half a byte, or 4 bits, which can represent a number between 0 and 15. And that number is used to select one of 16 possible palettes for that pixel. So for each pixel on the screen, the palette memory would tell the hardware which palette to select, and the screen memory tells the hardware which color in that palette to use. Don't worry if it doesn't make sense. There's no quiz coming later.

The addition of multiple palettes was a huge improvement! Now, up to 16 elements on-screen could have their own palette—256 colors just dedicated to that one element! This was exciting! I dove into writing code to support this feature in WTARG by adding functions to help artists manage multiple palettes and easily export them for inclusion in a game.

Mark added another feature that would get used a lot in future games: scaling, i.e. the ability to take an image and scale it down to any size. Without that feature, if we wanted something to seemingly move closer or further away, we'd have to save multiple copies of it at different sizes and have the game shift back and forth between them. And that took up memory. But scaling meant we could just store it at one size, freeing up a good amount of memory for other uses! Needless to say, the early '90s was an exciting time at Williams/Bally/Midway. *T2* and *Mortal Kombat* were both huge successes. The department was well-staffed with talented, driven, slightly eccentric—and sometimes crazy—people. Our hardware was top-notch. Our graphics were a far cry from most other games. Life was good.

THE DRIVING GAME

I've mentioned before that the time between projects is usually one of exploration. After *T2*, George Petro and Jack Haeger were looking at possible ideas for their next game, and one that came up was a driving game. There'd been a long history of driving games in the video game world, but none had involved digitized graphics, hardware scaling, and multiple palettes. We wondered if we could push the envelope.

So I set out to see what I could do. I'd never programmed a driving game before, and the idea of it seemed daunting. I had no idea how to generate a simple straight road, let alone curves or hills to make the terrain interesting.

Around this time, I was on a vacation out West with

my family, and I'd brought a video camera. At one point we were on a road in the middle of nowhere that had straightaways, curves, and hills in various combinations. With my wife driving, I started to videotape the road ahead for a long time, just to see if it might be useful later as reference footage.

Back at the office some days later, I watched the footage and looked for visual cues that I could use to algorithmically recreate the illusion of driving. I won't get into the details of the process. Believe me, I'd love to (this is what a geeky computer nerd loves doing), but the explanation would take up its own chapter. At any rate, after a little thinking and a brainstorm or two, I had some idea of how to algorithmically generate a very photo-to-realistic road using just one piece of digitized art: a 256-pixel square, repeatable piece of road.

I got the straightaway working first, and the results looked promising. Next I added curves, which wasn't all that difficult. I just had to skew each line of the road to the left or right by a different amount, and I'd figured out a way to compute that without resorting to trigonometry (which required too many CPU cycles to be practical). The truly challenging part was adding hills, but once I'd solved that, it looked kind of amazing.

Sadly, the driving game was scrapped while still in the exploratory stages. I'm not sure why. It may have been that George and Jack didn't have a concept for it that got them excited. Or maybe because Eugene had settled on a driving theme for his 3-D polygon game and the company didn't want another game competing against it. That driving game in question, *Cruis'n USA*, was still a year or two away at this point, despite management's hope that it'd be ready sooner. To his credit, Eugene wouldn't release it until he felt it was as good as it could be, schedules be damned!

MY HEAD GETS DIGITIZED

One day, artist Sal Divita came around and asked me to come to the blue screen studio with him. Didn't say why. I assumed there was some WTARG issue he wanted my help with. But when I got there, he told me to stand in front of the camera.

Sal was on the team (led by Mark Turmell) that created *NBA Jam*, another big success for the company. Now they were working on a follow-up, *NBA Jam Tournament Edition*. This version allowed players to enter their initials and birthday into the game, so that particular cabinet could store their statistics in its memory. What I didn't realize was that they were also pre-loading the game with records for most if not all of us who worked in the department. Not only that, but our records would be accompanied by our names and our heads on the players' bodies. Hence, my sudden photo shoot.

So I stood on a mark in our studio, turned in eight different directions, and got digitized into the new *NBA Jam TE*. I didn't think much of it at the time, but all these years later I kind of wish I'd been warned in advance so I could have made at least some attempt to look better on camera. I look like I'd just pulled an all-nighter. Come to think of it, it's entirely possible that I had. If you want to see for yourself, my initials are WBD and my birthday is 8/17. Anyway, after getting my head "shot," I just went back to work. It really wasn't until months later that I could appreciate what they had done. I'd go into an arcade and plop a quarter on the edge of an *NBA Jam TE* control panel to reserve my place. Then, after I'd entered my initials and birthday, the other players would see that my name appeared where the basketball player's name usually goes, with my head on the player's body! They'd inevitably stop dead in their tracks, give me a strange look, and say something like, "Wha??? How'd you do that?"

I still do that from time to time, even now. Who would have guessed there'd still be so many *NBA Jam TE* cabinets in arcades today? Sadly, I barely resemble the head on the player's body anymore.

RIDING THE RAPIDS

Not only did my name and head get to appear in *NBA Jam*, but my voice can be heard in at least one pinball machine. Dennis Nordman, my collaborator on *Us vs. Them*, had come over to Williams from Bally, where he was becoming quite the successful pinball designer. He was working on one particular game and needed someone to voice the main character. Naturally, I was happy to do it. And so I became the voice of Wet Willie in the game *White Water*. Yes, that's me screaming, "WHIIITE WAAATERRRRRRRR!" and many other lines. I seem to find this game at a lot of arcades and barcades even today—sometimes, sadly, with the sound turned down.

A lot of us who worked at Williams, artists and programmers alike, supplied voices for our games. Strangely, I usually didn't. *White Water* was a rare exception. I do remember my voice being used for a shuffle alley once, but I can't remember which one.

HANGIN' WITH ROCK STARS

George and Jack eventually settled on their next game. They decided to keep the *T2* team pretty much together, so Dozer and I would program along with George as lead while Jack led the art team, consisting of John Vogel and two new team members: Steve Beran and Marty Martinez. Once again, it was a shooting game with a gun controller. But this time the theme was very different: music was your weapon.

The original title was *Generation X*, but it soon became the more dynamic *Revolution X*. The premise was that the government had been overthrown and replaced by the New Order Nation, an oppressive regime led by the villainous Mistress Helga. The New Order Nation banned all music, as well as video games, TV, and (for some reason) magazines. The player was part of an uprising dedicated to restoring freedom. In addition to bullets, you had a button on the side of your gun that let you shoot CDs at your enemies.

The plan was to feature a real, hopefully famous band to play the role of guru/mentor to the player. Early on in the game, Mistress Helga crashes an illegal concert and abducts the band members, and a side goal of the game is to find and free them.

It was a challenge finding an iconic band that was willing to be part of the game. George and Jack wanted Aerosmith, which was kind of a pie-in-the-sky idea. Aerosmith was at the height of their popularity. Still, George and Jack videotaped a pitch for *Revolution X* and sent it to Aerosmith through the band's management company. Amazingly, the band responded with a big yes, and the details were worked out. The band would come to our blue screen studio to be digitized, and each member would be hidden throughout the game for players to rescue. Several Aerosmith songs would also be incorporated into the game.

Not that I was involved in any of that. I was off working on WTARG and the aforementioned driving game while all the groundwork was being laid. The scope of the game was pretty big. There were many locations and many characters to be digitized. Unlike *T2*, we couldn't just go to Hollywood and digitize stuff that already existed. The art team had to make every object, every prop, every costume piece from scratch. And while the overall design of the game was George and Jack's, I managed to make some contributions.

I've always been fascinated with creating depth in a video game; specifically, giving the illusion that the video game screen is a window into a three-dimensional world. Nowadays, that's pretty much the norm, and most hardware and tools are designed to make it very easy to implement. But back in those 2D days, it was still something of a dream. It should be noted that programmers were finding ways to make 3D polygon games on PCs at this time (e.g. *Wolfenstein 3D*), but the CPU time required to do all of the calculations meant the environments had to be very simple, and the early games ran very slowly. Meanwhile in the arcade world, Eugene was still trying to get his 3D polygon arcade system ready for prime time, so I was stuck with a 2D system.

All I'd ever worked on were 2D systems where we were essentially painting onto a flat, blank canvas. So the only way to achieve the effect I wanted was with a variety of tricks. With *Q*bert*, it was the optical illusion of the cubes. With *Us vs. Them* and *Exterminator*, it was a variation on the *M.A.C.H. 3* display system, which used perspective and different-sized images. *T2* used a small number of discrete planes. And then, most recently, there was the road-generation system I'd worked out for our driving game. All that software was designed to add a sense of depth to the player's experience. For our next game, I wanted to take that still a step further.

My goal was to create a development environment where you could place objects in a space, look at that space through a virtual camera, and control the way that camera moved through the space. The limitations were that the "camera" could only face in one direction, and all the objects were essentially flat billboards. We couldn't afford to do complex mathematical computations, so the camera couldn't rotate. It could only move forward, backward, up, down, and side to side. But it could move smoothly, seamlessly, and quickly.

I created a "world-building" tool that allowed artists to place elements of an environment into a virtual space and position the starting point of the camera. They could also define camera paths. All of this could be exported directly into the game with minimum effort on the part of whoever was building the world. This became our display system for *Revolution X*. One of its advantages was that the player could make directional choices. At any given location in a scene, the game could display, for example, a left and right arrow, and the player (by shooting one of those arrows) would be taken in that direction. In essence, we were creating multiple paths for a player to maneuver through a level. With the digitized members of Aerosmith hidden throughout the game, some paths might lead you to a band member, while alternate paths would not. This made rescuing all band members before the game was over an even greater challenge.

We were still limited by speed and memory, and those factors determined how big each of our worlds could be. In some cases we wanted fairly complex environments, and we might need to move from an exterior scene into a building. We didn't have the memory to store all of it at the same time, which meant some loading had to happen during gameplay. I hated the idea of having to cut to a "Loading" screen, which is what most games do. So I created a way to load a new world and free up the memory of the current world at the same time, while going through a door or via some other transition. You might notice this in *Revolution X* when entering the club or the building in the jungle. It's pretty seamless.

You may have noticed by now that a lot of what I'm most proud of in my career are technical achievements, things an average game player might not notice—under the hood stuff. I fully realize that while playing a game, no one really cares about that kind of thing. But it was my *job* to care about those details, because ultimately, making video games is about supplying people with an experience. A challenging but ultimately satisfying experience. I'm not saying *Revolution X* is a brilliant game by any means. Personally, I thought there was too much repetitive, non-strategic shooting. But my display system really had nothing to do with game design. It was a tool that could have been (and I hoped would be) used on many games to come. Unfortunately, that was not to be.

By far, the highlight of my whole experience making *Revolution X* was the Aerosmith shoot. It had been arranged for us to have them in our blue screen studio for three full days, during which we would digitize all of their animations for the game. Needless to say, everyone was incredibly excited at the prospect of having them on-site.

A view of our blue screen studio showing a mass of video and electronic equipment. (Chris Granner on left, John Vogel on right.)

Joe Perry gets his hair tended to.

Whatever you may think of their music (for the record, I was definitely a fan), they were at the height of their popularity at the time. Though I should add, Williams was not a stranger to having celebrities walk through its hallways. Every now and then, an actor would be hired to record lines for a pinball game based on a movie or TV show they'd been in. Once, Macaulay Culkin was in town shooting a movie and wanted to meet the guys who'd made *Mortal Kombat*, so he came by for a tour. But having Aerosmith here for three days was very different—special—and we all felt it.

George and Jack prepped tirelessly for days, putting together a shot list and getting the studio ready. The band requested certain types of food and drink (on the ultra-healthy side), and we made sure it was there. We had a green room set up where they could relax during downtime. We had a makeup person. We had a wardrobe area, although I'm pretty sure they brought their own costumes. We had a full crew made up of programmers, artists, technicians, and others who, for these three days, put their normal job duties on hold to perform some other function during the shoot. We were ready.

The anticipation was palpable as we waited for them that first day. When they arrived, it was a bit surreal. I remember thinking I was dreaming—it couldn't actually be possible that Aerosmith was here with us. But that feeling passed and we got down to business.

I was the clapboard guy. That means I'd write the current shot number on a clapboard and stick it in front of the camera before each shot. Even though WTARG had progressed to the point where we could shoot an animation live and see it on a game monitor within a minute or two, it made more sense to videotape everything for reference and digitize it later. Taping wasn't as crude a solution as it had been in the past because VHS tapes had been superseded by Hi8, which offered a 40 percent higher resolution. Plus, our Targa boards could take an S-VHS cable as input, which was an improvement over the traditional composite video signal since it resulted in less color bleeding. We occasionally digitized some shots in real time to see how they'd look in game. Depending on the result, we might keep what we had or re-shoot.

The band couldn't have been more down to earth. They were stoked to help, and they basically did everything George and Jack asked them to do. At some point each of the band members played

My job on set was to update and handle the clapboard. Here I am with Tom Hamilton.

Jack Haeger and Steven Tyler.

along as we piped their music over the loudspeakers. Lead singer Steven Tyler performed a variety of his signature moves with a mic stand. It was amazing!

Also in attendance at the shoot was Kerri Hoskins, a model who appeared in many Williams games because, aside from being stunningly beautiful, she was also a sweetheart and game for whatever was asked of her. She appeared as a cheerleader in *NBA Jam* and later showed off some martial arts skills as Sonya Blade in both *Mortal Kombat 3* and *4*. For *Revolution X*, she was almost unrecognizable as Mistress Helga, but that character was digitized at another time. During Aerosmith's visit, she played a cage dancer and prisoner wearing the smallest bikini I think I've ever seen. She also appeared in some shots with Steven Tyler. I never officially met her, as I wasn't usually involved with hiring or directing actors for our shoots. But it was a treat to see her work.

Despite the long days (thirteen hours each, as I recall), the shoot was light and fun. I remember during a break, guys were calling their wives and girlfriends and saying, "Hold on. Someone wants to talk to you." Then they'd put Steven Tyler on the phone and he'd chat with them while you could feel the stunned reaction all the way through the phone line. Another perk of having Aerosmith in the game was that we were all invited to one of their concerts in the Chicago area. It was part of the "Get a Grip" tour. I brought my wife and we had a great time. The band was in top form.

Aerosmith's visit also gifted me with my one and only celebrity urination story. Maybe some of you have a story like it. You're standing at a urinal, doing your business, and you notice that the guy standing next to you is famous. In my case, it was bassist Tom Hamilton, who happened to enter the bathroom right after me and proceeded to chat while we were emptying our bladders. I don't normally talk to anyone while I'm peeing, much less famous rock stars, so it was another surreal moment in what was fast becoming a whole scrapbook of surreal moments.

After the shoot, George and Jack pored over the footage to make sure we had everything we needed. Some shots didn't turn out as expected, and two of the band members came back the following week for a day of re-shoots. All of the behind-the-scenes proceedings (not including bathroom encounters) were videotaped and some of the footage was used for promotional material. You can find parts of it online. I wish I knew where the rest was.

With all the exciting stuff over, we had to finish making the game. I was responsible for a couple of the levels—one was a pretty large and complex jungle level, in which I managed to create a role for myself. When you first enter the Evergreen Chemical building, some dweeb behind the desk ducks down and starts lobbing grenades at you. That's me! I'm the dweeb! This cameo was another attempt of mine to insert a strategy puzzle into the game. No matter how much you shoot at my arm as it pops up and tosses a grenade, you will never get me to stop. The solution, by the way, is to shoot the three chains holding up the Evergreen Chemical sign above the desk. Once the last chain is destroyed, the last piece of the sign falls down and my character is crushed, with legs comically splayed upward. Cute, though during play testing I got worried whenever I saw people get to this spot and just shoot and shoot, accomplishing nothing. My thought (and hope) was that once someone figured it out, they'd tell other people about it so it would slowly filter through the playing community.

There were two versions of *Revolution X* built for the arcades: a two-gun cabinet and a three-gun cabinet. The three-gun cabinet was massive and extremely heavy. At the time *Revolution X* was released, I was a member of the Griffin Theatre Company in Chicago, and they were holding a benefit. One of the perks of being a game developer at Williams was they let us buy the games we worked on for a nominal cost (something like $100). I already had a *Q*bert*, a *Lotto Fun*, and a *T2* at home, and I really didn't have room for another arcade game. So I bought a three-gun *Revolution X* from Williams and donated it to the Griffin Theatre to auction off at their benefit. It sold for around $2,000, which was great for the theater, though I have no idea who bought it or how they got it home.

Revolution X was released in the early summer of 1994 to slightly less enthusiasm than *T2*. Some of that was to be expected, since the game concept was original and not based on a hugely popular movie that guaranteed a built-in audience. But I have to confess, I was still a little surprised at how well-received it was. I wasn't sure if Aerosmith would be that much of a draw for arcade game players. I mean, making *T2* into a shooting game was a natural fit, but Aerosmith and shooting? Or Aerosmith and video games, for that matter? And the concept was so wacky and out there. Weaponized music CDs? Mistress Helga? But it sold reasonably well and got rave reviews for the gameplay, graphics, and soundtrack. *GamePro* said: "*Rev X* is not a revolution in gun games, but it's definitely the best one yet."

Unfortunately, the game didn't translate well to the home systems of the day. Virtually all of its ports were widely panned, in some cases because the home system versions had the players use gamepad controllers instead of light guns, and that made their movements sluggish. Some criticized how a few of the home system versions toned down the more adult nature of the arcade version. From my perspective, though, that was good. It meant the arcade systems still offered something that home systems couldn't.

But that wouldn't last for long.

CHAPTER ELEVEN

LAST DAYS IN THE FUNHOUSE

With *Revolution X* behind me, the natural question became, as it did after every project: "What's next?"

My thoughts were leaning towards becoming the lead on a game of my own design. Up until then during my tenure at Williams, the only time I'd come close to being a lead on a game was with *USSA*, and that hadn't worked out so well. To be clear, I had no regrets about working under George and Jack on *T2* and *Rev X*. They were more than capable and great to work with, and I thoroughly enjoyed being part of those teams. But as we all pondered what our next steps might be, I felt it was time for me to take on some greater responsibility by heading up a game of my own.

Unlike Gottlieb, where my success with *Q*bert* gave me carte blanche to work on anything I liked, I was still something of an unproven asset at Williams when it came to game design. My personal taste in games leaned toward the surreal and absurd, and away from the violent and emotionally intense. Williams games (all of which, by this point, carried the Midway name) were generally on the high testosterone side, even if they sometimes embraced comedy and the surreal. Plus, the policies at Williams weren't the same as the early days at Gottlieb; concepts had to be presented and approved before moving forward. In order to be considered as a lead, I'd have to pitch game concepts directly to management—ones that would not only appeal to me, but also capture their interest and fit in with their idea of what a Midway game should be.

Since arcade game graphics had progressed to the point where we could use actors and tell stories, I thought about what genres might be fun to explore—preferably something that hadn't been done much. I'd always been a fan of scary movies. Monster movies, in particular. I'd practically grown up on them, from the old Universal monster movies they constantly showed on TV during my youth to the newer, more sophisticated brand of scary movies coming out in theaters at that time. I loved monster movies so much that if I couldn't convince any of my friends to see them with me, which was pretty often, I'd go see them by myself.

The thought struck me—and almost instantly seemed obvious—that I should come up with a horror-themed game! It fit the bill perfectly! The only horror-themed video arcade game I'd ever seen was *Chiller*, a light gun game released by Exidy in 1986. The goal of the game was to torture and murder innocents within a variety of stereotypical horror film environments (a torture chamber, a graveyard, etc.). Though the graphics were crude, they were still pretty disgusting. It was basically a torture porn game, and I think most people found it offensive and inappropriate for arcades.

I had no interest in creating anything disturbing or disgusting, but the field was wide open for something creepy and eerie. So I wrote up a design document for a game I called *Lair of the Undead*, a vampire-themed game with all sorts of other monsters thrown in for fun. My hope was to combine traditional arcade shoot-'em-up elements with interactive storytelling techniques. Your control would be a joystick with a trigger that allowed you to shoot a variety of weapons. Mostly wooden stakes, although you'd have opportunities to switch to other weapons, such as a machine gun loaded with silver bullets for werewolves. I was beyond excited about this concept, and thought the potential for what we could accomplish graphically with costumes and makeup would be very cool.

I have vague memories of the pitch meeting. Despite

ENEMIES AND GAME FLOW

Part 1 - Cemetery

The game opens as the players enter the gates of the cemetery with the mansion looming in the distance. Trees rustle, and the wind howls. The cemetery stretches out in all directions. The player's first goal is to get into the house. This is not so easy as the player will encounter assorted monsters on the way. Zombies will rise out of graves. Fully animated skeletons will appear out of statues. Harmless vagrants will morph into fully animated werewolves. One path will take you to a run-in with a gang of biker vampires. Some creatures will be easy to kill, others will require specific weapons (i.e. guns with silver bullets for werewolves), some areas of the game will be lockdown points where the player has to overcome a particular challenge or small boss creature. Action will be fierce, and just about everything in sight will respond to player fire.

The players will be able to move anywhere they like in the cemetery. Occasionally, they will come upon mausoleums, which they can explore. Some mausoleums have hidden rooms, some have underground passages connecting them to other mausoleums. One or two may even bring the player into the basement of the mansion! (But these will be extremely difficult for a novice to discover)

If the player reaches the house from above ground, he will be confronted with a moat and no bridge. But there will be a way to cross it if you can find it. There will also be creatures lurking in the water.

Part 2 - The Mansion

Once inside the house, the players must explore to find the vampire. What they will discover through creatures they encounter is that the vampire lives in a secret wing of the mansion. To enter it, they must find three keys and the hidden entrance.

Exploration becomes critical. Go up the grand stairway in front of you, or enter one of the doors on either side? The house contains hallways and doors. Beware passing by windows, as creatures may crash through at any moment. Any room can be entered. Some contain sultry scantily clad vampiresses with a taste for your blood. Some contain secret passages or powerups. Some contain innocents in danger who you can save. Any object may become unexpectedly alive and attack. Some rooms contain traps and pitfalls which you must spot or overcome.

As enemies attack you, your energy depletes. However, you will find items that will restore your energy partially or give you temporary invincibility. All the while you

- 4 -

After *Revolution X*, I wrote a proposal to do a horror-themed game, but management wasn't interested. In 1996, Sega came out with *House of the Dead* and it was a huge hit.

being pretty nervous, I did my best to sell it. Unfortunately, management wasn't all that impressed, and it never got off the ground. Maybe the horror genre seemed too risky, as it had never produced a hit game. Maybe my design wasn't fleshed out enough for their liking. Maybe my pitch just sucked, or maybe they had something else in mind for me and wanted my schedule to remain open. All of these are conjecture. I really don't know why they passed. Ironically, a couple of years later, *The House of the Dead*, a first-person shooter from Sega pitting the player against hordes of zombies, became a huge arcade hit.

INTO THE HIGHLANDS

My disappointment was short-lived, however. Some time later, management pitched an idea to me. Unlike the football game I'd been "asked" to work on years before, this was actually something to my liking. Apparently, some series of events unknown to me had led the producers of the *Highlander* TV series to connect with Williams, and the two parties entered into discussions about making a *Highlander*-based video game.

The original *Highlander* movie, released in 1986, was one of my favorites. If you're not familiar with the mythology, it's the story of Connor MacLeod (played by Christopher Lambert), a sixteenth-century Scottish Highlander who dies in battle and then comes back to life. He discovers he is one of a rare number of people throughout history who are immortal; now he will remain the same age and never die unless someone cuts off his head. When one of these immortals kills another, the victor absorbs the energy of the beheaded opponent in an event known as "the Quickening." This drives the different immortals to challenge each other to sword fights to the death throughout centuries—until "the Gathering," when the last few immortals left will fight until there's only one left, a victor who will gain "the Prize."

The film spawned several sequels, starting with *Highlander II: The Quickening* in 1991. The following year, a TV show spin-off debuted starring Adrian Paul as Duncan MacLeod, another member of the Clan MacLeod born roughly half a century after Connor who also turns out to be immortal. The TV series centered around Duncan trying to lead a simple, peaceful life, but frequently getting involved in protecting people from criminals or having to fight villainous immortals. The producers of that series were the ones talking to Williams. At the time, the show was about to enter its third season. In addition, a *Highlander* cartoon series was in production and about to hit television, and the new film sequel *Highlander: The Final Dimension* (originally titled *Highlander III: The Sorcerer*) was about to hit theaters. The hope was that, with all of this happening, maybe there was enough momentum for a video game to really take off.

Management, though, had some doubts. For one thing, the movie and film franchises were produced by different entities, so we wouldn't be able to use anything from the films, just the TV show. Plus, management wasn't sure how much life the TV show had left. We needed about a year's lead time before a game could realistically be done, and what if the show got canceled in that year? Finally, to take advantage of our digitized graphics, we'd want access to the actual actors from the series, but the producers couldn't guarantee their participation. Though I wasn't involved in the negotiations in any way, I have to assume this came down to money—how much the cast members would be paid, and who would pay for it.

So while the idea of a *Highlander* video game was

intriguing, it was far from a done deal. As a *Highlander* fan, I was totally on board. I felt like there was potential here to take an existing genre (the fighting game) and put a wrinkle on it that was new (swordplay). All with our amazing movie-like graphics and connection to a franchise whose popularity I believed was underestimated. Of course the devil's in the details, so I would have to get the look and feel of sword fighting absolutely right.

But while I loved the idea of being associated with this franchise and appreciated the technical challenges involved, I had my own concerns, primarily about the nature of the mythology. After all, it's a story about people who have to *cut each other's heads off.* If you recall, I'd gotten into a blisteringly heated discussion about *NARC* just by suggesting that it might not be so great if young children in arcades were exposed to that game's graphically violent images. Now here I was, considering making a game where the player would be asked to cut off someone's head with a sword.

Ultimately, I felt it was justified in the same way wounding cops in the knee was in *T2*—the game is based on an existing story, and if we're adapting it into a game, then that's the story we need to tell. But I wanted to make any beheadings in the game bloodless, so as to render them (hopefully) unrealistic. Granted, times had changed. Years after arcade owners had decided *Chiller* was too much for them, the world now had *Mortal Kombat* and there seemed to be a new standard for what was acceptable graphically in an arcade game. But instead of pushing that envelope further, I was happy to take a step back from it and willing to gamble that it would still be fun.

While management continued their talks with the show's producers, I set my sights on figuring out the technical elements of the game. Specifically, how to make a satisfying sword battle. By either fate or good fortune, one of our own programmers, Jake Simpson, happened to be a bit of a swordsman, so he became the actor for my experiments. I digitized him in a variety of poses, doing different offensive and defensive moves at enough angles to allow for smooth motion when the player character moved or turned. Next, I wrote some code to have the player control one instance of Jake while facing off against a second computer-controlled instance of him. As always, my aim was to add a third dimension to what was traditionally a two-dimensional view, so that in this world, the players could rotate around each other as desired. It was a crude experiment, but watching Jake circle around and then attack himself was both comical and helpful. I felt pretty confident I could get the look and feel of combat working the way I wanted when we brought in actors for the real game.

Here's where the story gets a little weird. Despite my desire to have bloodless beheadings, management began to push back on the game's violence.

They'd ask, "Do you have to cut your enemy's head off? Isn't there something a little less extreme we could do?"

And I'd say, "Uh . . . no! It's part of the mythology. It's what makes this *Highlander* and not a bunch of random guys trying to kill each other with swords."

After *T2* and now two *Mortal Kombat* games, this sudden squeamishness confused me. But it was the backlash and controversies attached to those very same games that had started wearing management down. They were looking to distance themselves from any similar or potentially worse criticism and trouble in the future. I began to worry that I would lose their support and the whole deal would fall through.

A TOUGH CHOICE

Meanwhile, other things were going on in my life that were tempting me to contemplate something I'd never seriously considered before—a move from Chicago to Los Angeles.

I'd been living in Chicago for over a decade, and I loved it there. I'd gotten married there. My children had been born there and were attending school there. I found Chicago to be an extremely livable and pleasant city. The winters didn't really bother me; they weren't much different from my childhood winters in New York City.

So what did Los Angeles have to do with anything? Well, it had to do with acting. Over the years, I'd been acting more and more in local theater productions, commercials, industrial films, and a couple of independent feature films. It was something I did mostly for fun and in my off-hours, since I was perfectly happy with my day job making video games. But during that time, I'd gotten to know and work with many actors who were serious about acting as a career. As they were moving up the proverbial ladder—taking bigger roles in larger, more prestigious theaters and becoming known to more people in the acting community—I sort of moved along with them. In 1994, some of those friends were looking at a move to Los Angeles, since Chicago had limited opportunities for film and TV at the time. And those friends were of the opinion that I should think about moving to L.A. as well.

I can't say I'd never thought about it, but I was happy not just with my job, but my entire life in Chicago. Looking at the big picture, I couldn't find a compelling reason to move. But then things started happening that made me question my stance, and they all seemed to happen at once. The inability to get a signed deal with the *Highlander* TV producers was one of those things.

Another was management's hesitation to commit to developing a potentially violent game, despite my pledge to keep it less graphic than what was already out there. I was also becoming aware of a shift happening in the arcade industry.

For my entire career, arcade hardware had been superior in every way to home game systems. But in the 1990s, that tide was starting to turn. Graphics cards for PCs were becoming capable of images as good as or surpassing most arcade hardware. And the industry was moving away from digitized 2D graphics and embracing polygons as the wave of the future, with polygonal systems becoming the norm in both arcades and homes. I believed the arcade industry was heading for another crash, although I couldn't know how bad it would be or how long it would last. But as PC graphics got better, I suspected that the allure of arcades would die, and people would play more at home. And, as a side note, it just so happened that a lot of home game development was going on in—you guessed it—Los Angeles.

As my thoughts drew me to seriously contemplate a move to L.A., I began to think of the practical considerations. First and foremost, I had to discuss this with my wife and see if she'd be on board. I also had to think about taking my kids out of school and away from their friends. I had to think about the logistics of selling my house in Chicago and buying one in L.A., a city I didn't know well. It was daunting. But the seeds were there, and the mental gears were turning. Committing to a move without knowing what would await us just seemed crazy. But going to L.A. for a few months to scope things out and see if it could work, well, that seemed . . . doable. I spent the early part of December preoccupied with these thoughts to the point of distraction. To move or not to move, that was the question. But the answer was not forthcoming.

December dragged on and I grew more and more discouraged about the *Highlander* game ever getting a green light. Talks seemed to have stalled completely. I was becoming pessimistic about ever being able to make another arcade game—if, in fact, the arcade industry managed to survive. But a positive ray of hope presented itself in the form of a play audition with a theater company that had been getting a lot of praise and publicity. Working with that company could lead to some attention and more auditions for film and TV shows that came to Chicago. Getting cast would certainly be a great reason to put all this Los Angeles nonsense behind me and commit to staying in Chicago a while longer.

So I scheduled the audition, and at the same time, made kind of a bold and insane promise to myself. If I booked this play, I would stay in Chicago. If I didn't, I would quit my job and go to Los Angeles for four months to see if a permanent move made sense. It was a ballsy plan, but at least it meant I'd finally have a direction for what to do with my life.

The audition went well from my perspective, but the reaction of the people I auditioned for was so cold and dismissive, I left the audition thinking—no, *knowing* with a deep certainty—that I hadn't gotten the role. "Okay," I thought to myself as I walked out of the theater. "Looks like I'm going to Los Angeles!" That decision instantly brought with it a sense of peace and clarity. The next day, I went into Williams and gave notice.

I think everyone was kind of shocked. I was a little shocked myself. Quitting my job was a real leap of faith that there was something worth moving to in L.A. Looking back, it seems like a crazy thing to do, but in the moment it just felt right. A little scary if I thought about it too much, but right. I agreed to stay on at Williams to clean up and document any code I was working on so it could be handed over to someone else. Then, in two weeks' time, I'd be leaving.

But the universe decided to test me. That evening, I heard from a friend in the theater company that I'd gotten the part in the play after all.

Time stopped. I tried to process this news, but I couldn't because it seemed completely impossible. I was so sure they hadn't liked my audition! I must've stood with my mouth agape for what seemed like an eternity. Eventually I managed to spit out, "But I'm going to Los Angeles. I just quit my job today." I turned the role down.

A part of me started to panic. Had I made the right choice?

Then, a couple days later, I arrived at work to find Neil Nicastro, president and CEO of Williams, waiting for me in my office. Though I knew him better than I'd ever known Boyd Browne, president of Gottlieb, my interactions with him were rare. And in my almost ten-year history with Williams, he had never ever, not once, come to my office.

He said, "Warren, you'll never guess what's happened. We've reached an agreement with the producers of *Highlander*. Not only that, they've given us everything we asked for. Including shooting time with the actors. All you have to do is say yes, and we'll sign it, and it's a go."

Once again, I had kind of an out-of-body experience hearing this. Was this real? All the things I'd told myself would keep me in Chicago were suddenly happening. And it wasn't too late to change my mind. I could have said, "Great! Let's do it!" and not skipped a beat. Instead, I found myself saying, "I'm so sorry, Neil, but I'm going to Los Angeles." This time, there was no panic, just calm. I have to say, he took it very well.

I've described in these pages most of the difficult decisions I'd made throughout my life, but I never felt the universe conspiring to tempt me into changing my mind more than I did then. And by not giving in to that temptation, I knew I'd made the right choice.

Although the *Highlander* game wasn't in the cards for me, I hoped someone else might take on the project, because I believed in the concept. In fact, I was pretty convinced management would have no problem finding someone to pick it up and complete it. But the game never got made. Either no one else at Williams was interested, or maybe management felt they had dodged a bullet and let it go when I left. Interestingly, other companies have tried making *Highlander* games over the years, but those that managed to get released haven't been particularly successful. Maybe someday.

January arrived and with it, my last day at Williams. A bunch of the guys from the video department took me out to lunch at my favorite Thai restaurant, Opart Thai in Lincoln Square. It was a large group of artists, programmers, and techies who came to send me off, and I was both humbled and honored by the company I was in. I really admired everyone in this group.

It's hard to describe what it was like to be working among those people at that time. The level of talent and commitment was huge, although we certainly weren't patting ourselves on the back and telling everyone how great we were. Outside of the coin-op industry, we were pretty much anonymous. Even within the industry, none of us were treated like rock stars, although some names like Eugene Jarvis and Steve Ritchie were known.

Back then, everyone was working at the top of their form, inspired only by a desire to make something cool. And we inspired each other to up our game, even if sometimes it was driven by a spirit of friendly competition. Mostly, though, we were competing with ourselves, what we'd done as a company, and what we saw the rest of the industry doing. I don't think any of us thought about the lasting effects of our work. We were just having fun. And while we were each driven by our own motivating factors, the result was pretty much a well-oiled machine that delivered some outstanding games into the world.

Now, it's certainly possible that I'm looking at the past through rose-colored glasses, but even acknowledging that the Williams/Bally/Midway family may have had some dysfunctional elements doesn't take away from the end results.

As for the fate of arcades, they did in fact experience a decline for a few years until they were rejuvenated slightly by *Dance Dance Revolution*, which brought players back for a unique experience they couldn't get at home. The first time I saw people playing *DDR* in an arcade, I smiled. I felt hopeful that the arcade experience would never truly fade away, because people are social animals and want to be around each other. And I felt a little ashamed that I didn't trust that more.

In retrospect, my timing for leaving was pretty good. Williams would carry on for a few more years, enjoying the success of growing the Midway brand for the home market, and then becoming a manufacturer of slot machines. But the pinball division lasted only until 1999, and they stopped making video arcade games in 2001. I was crushed when I heard of both these events, but the demise of the pinball division hit me especially hard. While I knew there would still be a video arcade industry—even if it would be smaller than in its heyday—it seemed that pinball might actually become permanently extinct.

Thankfully, that never happened.

CHAPTER TWELVE

LOOSE ENDS

The focus of this book was always intended to be my years making games in the coin-op industry. And while I couldn't know for sure when I left Chicago that I would never again make another video arcade game, don't cue up the sad music just yet. My story, and my video game career, didn't stop there. The move to Los Angeles began a decade working in the PC and console game market.

While there are many stories to tell about those years, they will have to wait for another time. Still, there are some events worthy of a mention, most having to do in some way with my coin-op days.

UNEXPECTED NOSTALGIA

I arrived in Los Angeles in January of 1995, one year to the day after the infamous Northridge Earthquake. Though I had no actual job during this time, I was generously allowed to continue working on WTARG from California. This was due to the kindness of Paul Dussault. An engineer at Williams before I ever worked there, Paul had left the company and then come back years later as a manager. When I gave notice, he agreed to a part-time arrangement that provided me with some income while I was away. So I continued to develop and improve

WTARG, converting it from its roots as a DOS program to run on an operating system that had recently become quite popular called Windows. The release of Windows 3.1 in 1992 really caused the fledgling operating system to catch on with the masses. By 1995, I felt like moving WTARG to Windows was long overdue.

I returned to Chicago that spring, as intended, and I was encouraged enough by my experience in L.A. to want to go back for another exploratory visit in September. During that summer in Chicago, I became aware of something brewing in the world that I never would have expected.

Somehow, a *Q*bert* fan had found my e-mail address and contacted me. He asked if I could write up a short history of the development of *Q*bert* that he could post online. I obliged, and he posted it. That history has moved over the years, but still exists at www.coinop.org/features/qbstory. A slightly edited version of it also appears in Van Burnham's book, *Supercade*.

I thought his contacting me was such an odd and unique thing that when I learned he lived just a couple of hours south of me, I invited him and his girlfriend to come up and see my *Q*bert* cabinet at home, which was running *Faster Harder More Challenging Q*bert*. It had been over a decade since anyone had seen *FHMC Q*bert* anywhere, so it was a pretty rare opportunity and I thought he would enjoy it. (This was before those ROMs were released to MAME.)

He agreed and soon after, he and his girlfriend came by for a visit. We had a thoroughly lovely time. As we spoke, I was initially surprised by the level of affection he had for what was, from my perspective, an old forgotten game. Gradually, the realization hit me that his affection made perfect sense. Nostalgia tends to happen in generational cycles. All the kids who played that first wave of video games in the '70s and '80s were growing into young adults with a fondness for the happy memories of their childhoods. Not only that, but there was this "new" thing called the internet that allowed them to create online groups and connect with others with similar interests, to share their thoughts and feelings.

This appreciation for work I'd done years ago took me by surprise, but was also very rewarding. I didn't often think about my work leaving any lasting impression on society. My goal in everything I did was generally to please myself and hopefully entertain people, but it never occurred to me that any game I worked on would be memorable over time. As I said goodbye to my guests, I couldn't really predict the extent to which I would be surprised again and again in the coming years.

With only the slightest awareness on my part, the retro-gaming movement had begun.

L.A. STORIES

My return to Los Angeles in September was intended to be four months, but turned out to be eight. The extra time was needed, because once I decided to make the move permanent, I had to do mundane things like find a house and a job.

The job I found was with Disney Interactive, the division of Disney where home video games were produced. I worked in the tools group, developing support software for artists as needed. Thanks to a colleague, John Palmer, I was turned on to a new algorithm for color reduction and palette generation, the Wu algorithm. This generated far better results than any of the algorithms I'd uncovered years before. It was first published in 1992, so if I'd known of its existence, I could have conceivably added it to WTARG. I wish I'd known about it while I was still at Williams.

At some point during my time with Disney, the Academy of Interactive Arts and Sciences was created. I became a founding member. This organization was an attempt to elevate the status of video games to that of movies, which has been represented for many decades by AMPAS, the Academy of Motion Picture Arts and Sciences. Time has certainly proven this move to be a reasonable one, and AIAS still exists today. I remember going to one of their first awards shows. It was held in a Downtown L.A. theater, and had some minor celebrities as host and presenters. DI was up for some awards, and I think we may have even won a couple. Although it was a far cry from the glitz, glamour, and media event that is the Oscars, it was kind of fun. I never dreamed I'd see the video game industry attain such prestige.

THE RETURN OF Q*BERT

Working for Disney Interactive had some perks, and one was being sent to the annual Game Developers Conference in northern California. The GDC was a place for game developers to come together and share information on all aspects of the industry. There were panels on every game-related subject imaginable, as well as an exhibit hall and a job fair. The GDC started out humbly in 1988, attended by just a few game designers, but grew rapidly to an attendance of 4,000 in 1996. By contrast, the 2019 GDC was attended by a record 29,000 people!

At one particular GDC towards the end of the millennium, I found myself wandering around the job fair and noticed that Sony Computer Entertainment of America (SCEA) had a booth. Knowing that Sony had inherited the rights to Q*bert when it bought Columbia Pictures, and being aware of the recent interest in old arcade games—after all, Hasbro Interactive had recently put out a PC version of Frogger—I went up to one of the guys from Sony and introduced myself. I asked him, "Why haven't you guys done anything with Q*bert?"

He seemed puzzled. "What do you mean?""Well," I said, "you own the rights to Q*bert and there's a real interest in some of these old arcade games. It seems weird that you haven't brought Q*bert back."

His eyes seemed to glaze for just a moment. "Wait . . . we own the rights to Q*bert?"

"Yeah. Didn't you know that?"

He looked incredulous. "No!" He immediately started scribbling a note down on a pad of paper and called out to his colleagues at the booth. "Did you guys know Sony owns the rights to Q*bert?" They shook their heads, and an animated conversation ensued. They thanked me for letting them know. I offered my services in developing new games featuring the character, and they nodded but were lost in their own thoughts.

About a year later, Hasbro (under the banner Atari Interactive) released a PC remake of Q*bert. Naturally, I had no involvement. But I think it was at the next GDC that I ran into someone from Hasbro and struck up a conversation about the game. Once again, I offered to participate in advancing the character with some game play ideas I had. This time, the fellow seemed interested.

"That'd be great! We'd love to hear whatever ideas you have!"

"Sure!" I replied. "Let's get together some time and work out an arrangement."

"Oh . . . we couldn't hire you or pay you. But we'd love to hear your thoughts."

I can't remember the exact words I used in response.

They were kind, as I'm a kind person, but my thoughts were more along the lines of, "Are you fucking kidding me?"

Here's another *Q*bert*-related story that happened during my tenure at Disney.

The MAME (Multi Arcade Machine Emulator) project was taking off in the mid to late 1990s. MAME was a collection of software emulators that ran under Windows and would perfectly (or close to perfectly) emulate various arcade hardware from multiple manufacturers. Today, there are literally thousands of arcade games you can play under MAME. Back then, there were maybe a few hundred, and *Q*bert* was one of them. To get around copyright infringement, the emulators didn't come with any games. It was like having a hardware system with no ROMs plugged in. You had to search the internet to find ROM images of any games you wanted to play in order for it to work. Generally, though, those ROM images weren't too hard to find.

I was told about this by a Disney colleague named Fred Sookiasian. He was working in some capacity with the folks behind MAME and knew my arcade game history. I was pretty amazed at the amount of work that went into creating these emulators, all done as a hobby in people's spare time, and I was flattered that *Q*bert* was included. If this brought *Q*bert* back into people's consciousness, that was great.

It occurred to me that since the hardware was emulated, any game that ran on it would run in that emulator. So any other Gottlieb games—such as *Reactor*, *Krull*, or *Mad Planets*—would run, as would any unreleased games, as long as you had the ROMs. In fact, there was such as a game that I happened to have running in a cabinet at home that had never been released to the public: *FHMC Q*bert*.

I mentioned to Fred that I had an unreleased version of a new *Q*bert* game and suggested donating the ROM images for use with the MAME emulator. He was excited about it. *FHMC Q*bert* existed as a total of nine ROM chips. There were three program ROMs, two background block ROMs, and four foreground sprite ROMs. The sound ROMs were identical to the original *Q*bert*. I created file images of each ROM and handed them over to Fred, who passed them along to other people, who saw to it that they were posted online somewhere.

And thus, after about fifteen years of languishing in my home, *FHMC Q*bert* was finally unleashed into the world. I'm happy I was able to do that, but I still wish more people knew about it and would give it a try. I was thrilled to learn some years ago that hobbyists had developed circuit boards that allowed both the original *Q*bert* and *FHMC Q*bert* to co-exist in a cabinet, switchable via the control panel. I've also seen cabinets that are equipped with all three versions: original, *FHMC*, and *Qubes*. The ingenuity and passion of collectors is incredible and never ceases to amaze me.

THE 2000S

Disney Interactive suffered consistent layoffs while I was there. I managed to avoid losing my job for four years, but in 2000, I was informed that I'd be gone with the next wave. I was offered a transfer to Imagineering, which I jumped at. Working at Walt Disney Imagineering had always been one of my dream jobs! Sadly, it didn't turn out to be what I expected (a story for another book), and after four months, I regretfully left Disney. I started looking around for other jobs immediately, and that's how I got to meet Nolan Bushnell.

Bushnell is a legend in the video game world, mostly for co-creating Atari. When I heard that a company he'd started called uWink was looking for software engineers, I was very excited to interview there. During that interview, I ran into a familiar face. You may recall my story about how Premier passed on my doing a second game after *Exterminator* because a young programmer with no experience convinced them that he could do one faster and cheaper? Well that guy was now working for uWink. There were no hard feelings about it on my end; in fact, I was glad to see that my might-have-been protégé was doing well. But the job didn't seem like a good fit for me, so it didn't lead anywhere. But meeting Nolan briefly was a real treat.

Thanks to my former Disney colleague, Joel Goodsell, I eventually landed at a company called Check Six Studios. The project that Check Six was working on was a new Spyro the Dragon game—the fourth in the series, the first for the Playstation 2, and the first to not be created by Insomniac Studios.

The story of *Spyro: Enter the Dragonfly* is worthy of a book unto itself. Rather than get into it now, let's just say it was a bumpy couple of years, which resulted in a game that was something less than what we all wanted it to be. Oddly, I've been approached by a number of people lately wanting to know the story behind this game. I'm reminded of that time in the mid-'90s when people suddenly wanted to hear stories about the creation of *Q*bert* after years without anyone being interested. I guess, once again, the cycle of nostalgia seems to be coming due.

The next few years found me working mostly on console and PC projects that were fun and satisfying to work on, but never saw the light of day. One did, although its release was very limited. In 2008, I left the game industry and spent a couple of years working as an R&D engineer for Lucasfilm's Industrial Light and Magic. That was a dream job while it lasted, and I wish it had lasted longer.

PARTING THOUGHTS

Looking at the current state of the video game industry, I'm of two minds. On the one hand, I have to marvel at the technological leaps that have happened since I left the industry. The processing power of modern consoles is staggering compared to their predecessors of just a decade ago. Advances in simulations of hair, water, fabric, and fire allow for a photo-realism in games that makes the original *Mortal Kombat* look painfully crude. And the simulation of humans in games has evolved to the point where we're on the verge of overcoming the "uncanny valley" effect.

On the other hand, these advancements aren't a surprise to those of us who've been around a long time. The future was always sitting far off on the horizon. We couldn't see it clearly, but we knew it was there. And we knew we'd get there; we just didn't know when.

I'm probably most excited by the development of virtual reality technology, which is something I've dreamed about for years. Stereo-vision glasses (more commonly known as 3D) have been around in the world of video games for a long time. Like LaserDiscs, they just weren't ready for prime time. And a number of arcade games were released with some sort of 3D ability, but it never seemed to catch on. Once, back at Gottlieb, a dentist from Florida was brought in for a visit to demonstrate some new technology he'd developed. It used a standard monitor mounted flat and pointing upwards, much like a cocktail arcade cabinet, and required a user to wear electronic 3D glasses. Miraculously, the image on the screen seemed to sitting on top of the monitor in full 3D, much like the hologram of Princess Leia in the original *Star Wars*. Unfortunately, it was a single player experience and the field of view was very specific. The viewer couldn't move at all and had to be in a very specific spot. And due to the nature of the illusion, things couldn't really move too much around the screen. We couldn't figure out what to do with it, given its limitations. Still, it was cool to look at.

Modern virtual reality is nothing short of astonishing and immersive. And it's just in its infancy! The same can be said for its cousin, augmented reality. Once again, I can see something on the horizon for these technologies if they can remain viable in the marketplace. It's a concern considering how many people find VR uncomfortable and disorienting. But I can envision its applications not just for games but for education,.presentations, travel, and more.

Strangely, the emergence of retro-gaming events (and to a lesser extent, e-sports) surprised me way more than any technological breakthroughs. And yet, what a beautiful way to celebrate one's youth. When I go to retro-gaming shows, I see a lot of parents playing the old games with their children, sharing a part of their childhood and instilling a love for them in a new generation. These old, oddball games (by today's standards) seem just as popular today as they were thirty or forty years ago. I guess it's not much different from pinball. In a world saturated with video games, pinball games are a refreshing alternative. In a world filled with blockbuster triple-A titles with deep stories and cinematic graphics, games like *Q*bert* and *Pac-Man* are a refreshing alternative.

In the 2000s, when phones with LCD screens started to come out, a lot of arcade game developers from back in the day found themselves with a new medium to explore. The resolution on some of those early phones was pretty close to that of the standard 19-inch monitor in a video arcade game. So, a whole new market emerged for games with simple graphics and gameplay—no quarter-sucking required! As screens grew bigger, better, and denser, the games for those screens went the same route. Now, there really isn't a medium for simple low-res video games anymore. So people return to the games they love because, thankfully, they can. It's that feeling of nostalgia that makes us want to turn back the clock and remember a simpler time.

Believe it or not, I was never one for looking backwards. Writing this book has forced me to do so, and I can't help but feel fortunate. My career and life have been largely filled with events and relationships that I treasure, with doses of pain and disappointment along the way, as is the case more or less with any life. And while I'm happy to have set these memories down on paper for others to enjoy, I'm also gratified to leave a record of these experiences for those who may feel they're of some value. That's not for me to decide, though. I just happened to be there.

So now, with the task of writing this book behind me, I can again turn my gaze forward, looking ahead to the blank page that is tomorrow, and ask myself my favorite question in the world . . .

"What's next?"

Above: Jeff Lee, Howie Rubin, and me at the 2018 Pinball Expo.

Below: Although I'd seen both Jeff Lee and Dave Thiel occasionally over the years, the three of us had never been reunited in the same space until 2016 when I made a surprise visit to the Pinball Expo in Wheeling, IL. Jeff Lee picked me up and we drove up with O'Hare to surprise Dave Thiel, who didn't know I was coming. From left to right: me, Jeff, and Dave.

AFTERWORD

by John Newcomer
Creator of *Joust,* lover of design,
and lifelong member of the Warren Davis fan club

In *Creating Q*bert,* Warren Davis takes the reader on a journey through a uniquely inventive turning point in history. He brings to life not only his story of developing an iconic arcade game, but also shares his creative process and practical life lessons for aspiring game designers:

- Acknowledge your talents and find ways to expand them.
- Creativity comes in many forms; recognize your own, those of others, and what you can observe around you.
- Keep on this path and, when it's time to go to work, you'll find that you have a bigger collection of top-notch tools to use than you realized.
- Journeys often take unexpected twists and turns. You never know when your life will intersect with old acquaintances or complete strangers whose paths parallel yours.

Warren and I both started in the coin-op video industry at about the same time, in the early '80s. At that time, Chicago was *the* magical place to be for designing games in the U.S. Atari on the West Coast got the most press, but Chicago was the real epicenter.

Chicago had a long history of manufacturing coin-op pinball games and amusements, and the manufacturing facilities and workers who made those amusements were easily repurposed for the emerging arcade video industry. It was natural for Bally, Williams, Stern, and Gottlieb to branch into arcade video games.

One of the most important test locations in the country, Mothers (in the Chicago suburb of Mt. Prospect), was where most of the companies tested their video games just prior to release. This dominance of coin-op development brought the showcase trade shows, AOE and AMOA, to Chicago. Trade shows were opportunities to make magical connections.

Chicago was also the location of the most important toy-inventing think tank in the country, Marvin Glass and Associates. From the 1960s through the 1980s, toys and games were largely invented at these secretive studios. An early catalyst for the electronic game craze was the game *Simon*, created by Marvin Glass inventors Ralph Baer and Howard Morrison. Marvin Glass and Associates later started its own video group, which did *Tapper*, and eventually part of that team spun off to become Incredible Technologies.

When Warren and I first started in the coin-op video industry, he at Gottlieb and I at Williams/Midway, many of the "rock stars" who had created the big hits of 1980 and '81 now had special contracts and status. Companies needed a second wave of "work for hire" game creators, like Warren and me, who could keep the assembly lines moving with a cost-effective payroll. There was no manual on how to make a great game, or how to lead a team, or even how to figure out what the next great game would look like.

My path began as an Indiana country boy who got an Industrial Design degree and came to Chicago to work for Gordon Barlow, a senior partner at Marvin Glass who had started his own inventing studio. I went to Mothers to have fun and see what was new just like any other twenty-something guy would, and knew immediately when I saw my first video game that this could change the course of entertainment. I started looking for ways to transition into the coin-op video game industry.

In November '81 there was a magical connection. A programmer I worked with at Barlow's talked about being invited to a party with other programmers in the area. I jokingly asked if he could get any tips on getting hired in coin-op. The next day, he came back and told me he'd met Tim Skelly at the party, who gave him the name of a headhunter and a general pay range for employees. I acted immediately, and got interviews and offers from Gottlieb and Williams, but accepted Ken Fedesna's offer with Williams.

The development and production of *Joust* and *Q*bert* overlapped quite a bit. After *Robotron* hit earlier in '82, many in the industry were saying that would be the last of the games that sold over 20,000 units. Many experts were proven wrong, as both games outsold *Robotron* by a few thousand. Having these three games hit in succession at a time when too many clones were pouring in was good for the industry.

When *Q*bert* was on test and *Joust* was in production, Williams' VP of sales knew most of the places every game company in the area tested their prototypes. He had an ex-pinball designer take pictures and do an analysis of *Q*bert*, which the VP showed me. Most of the concerns Warren outlined in this book were in that report. While my VP of sales was somehow worried about a competitor, my view was from the development trenches and I felt an instant kinship to Warren.

First of all, I thought: "Good for Gottlieb and the team lead for trying something new to give players a reason to come back to the arcade."

Next, I quoted *Q*bert*: "@!#?@!" x3. I have been a fan of M.C. Escher for years. At the time, I had three framed prints on my wall and I never made the connection to take that inspiration and create a game with it. "Good for the team lead for doing that!"

Many of Warren's accounts in this book hit home. Making a game in the early '80s was an adventure, but brutal. You had to live with so many limitations, and the "internet" of the time was a frayed library card, or conversations with fellow fans and creators without the convenient and instantaneous connections we have now. There was no extra memory for cut scenes, nor piled-on special effects, nor a wide variety of characters and backgrounds. Nothing would help you if the game's core was flawed.

The longer you worked on these games, the more you became emotionally invested, and now this idea germ was your baby and you wanted to protect it. At the end of the day, Warren or any team lead would be judged by the simple question: "Is it fun?"

The answer would be unbiased and honest: "Did you impulsively put in another quarter?" Yes, yes we did for *Q*bert*, and good for you, Warren and team, for making such a charming and addictive FUN game.

As the arcade industry was taking a nosedive, I got an unexpected call from a headhunter on behalf of Ron Waxman (who I had met when previously interviewing at Gottlieb) and Bill Adams (who, through another magical connection, I had met on a plane to Tokyo). Ron offered me a job, and I took it.

I did not work directly with Warren at Gottlieb/Mylstar, because we were both to lead or influence separate projects. But I wanted to know more about him. I had observed him on a couple of occasions, and one day I mentioned to Ron Waxman that I was curious about Warren. There was more to him than most programmers I knew in the games industry. Ron sat there puffing heavily on a big cigar while he pondered the answer for what felt like three pregnant pauses.

"Thespian . . . Warren loves the theater; programming is his day job."

That put Warren in perspective for me. Many programmers have tried to make a game, but most have been unsuccessful, especially at leading the endeavor. Warren's spark? He is an entertainer. Yes, he's considering the tech side, but he's also working as a director, producer, and actor, carefully contemplating story, character development, pacing, camera angles, and production. Having all these tools on his belt is a rare and wonderful thing.

Warren's scope is also one of his superpowers. Many game designers are like directors who, when they get a hit, milk the formula until it stops making money. That approach can succeed for a while, but there comes a point when players tire of the same formula and walk away looking for something fresh. So, taking a low-risk formula can become the biggest risk of all. The ability and willingness to try something new and tell a different story is admirable.

When Warren created *Us vs. Them*, he departed from his successful *Q*bert* format. That courageous path demonstrates Warren's love of story and a wider scope of entertaining.

When Gottlieb/Mylstar ceased operations, both Warren and I landed at Williams/Midway. The first project we created together was *USSA*. Learning a new system for making a game is gratifying, especially since both of us shared the view that these were stepping stones on the way to games becoming interactive movies.

Evolving a game was different for me. My toy-and-game-inventing roots usually followed a format of brainstorming, visualizing a direction, writing or sketching the idea so everyone can share a vision, then iterating and changing the vision when you hit a milestone.

When taking this new hardware for a spin, Warren's way proved to be more suitable. It was fun to see how things took shape, especially when Warren brought to life the ability to launch a rocket from your 4x4 and steer it. At that point I could easily see it as a complete story: *Red Dawn* meets Michael Nesmith's *Elephant Parts* "Neighborhood Nuclear Superiority" sketch. We both share the sting of that project being shut down, just as it was shaping up.

We worked together on *Revolution X* and on the *Highlander* pitch. I went on to co-design *High Impact Football* with Eugene Jarvis and Ed Boon, plus did some early work on *NBA Jam*. Although he did not work on these games directly, Warren's digitizing tools made their distinct visuals possible.

Everyone who was in the department at the time has stories about Warren's rock star talents and unassuming manner. While many game developers are drawn toward the spotlight, Warren sees the big picture and leads with his creative curiosity instead of his ego. He could easily head up a project, or could be equally happy as a support programmer, or as the digital alchemist creating custom software to make everyone more successful. One of his most notable contributions was realizing the potential of the rapidly improving hardware capacity and creating tools to utilize it. This gave Williams/Midway games a uniquely realistic animation quality that stood in brilliant contrast to other brands.

In an industry filled with some very smart people, creative diversity, and a range of personality types frequently under pressure, I can safely say that everyone I've met who knows Warren has the utmost respect for him and is grateful for his contributions in our wide range of games. His body of work from *Q*bert* through the Williams/Midway digitized era makes Warren Davis one of the most important figures in the early history of video games, and someone you should know.

ACKNOWLEDGMENTS

The notion of writing a book has always been pretty foreign to me, so to have finished one is nothing short of a miracle. Naturally, I could never have gotten to this point without help from many people, some in big ways, others in small but crucial ways.

First, I must thank Alan Sizzler Kistler, who provided guidance and expertise in editing and refining this book as it was being written. A talented author himself, he was patient and present during the two years it took for me to set all my memories down on paper.

I also want to thank Jeffrey Goldman and Santa Monica Press for responding to the book and offering to publish it, as well as providing notes to guide me through a revision process which I believe resulted in an improved version of the book. Additional improvements were due to the skillful editing efforts of Kate Murray. Her keen eye and excellent judgment resulted in many corrections and adjustments I never would have thought of. I'm extremely grateful for the care with which she approached my story.

I'd also like to thank the many colleagues I've seen over the past few years at retro-gaming events. The conversations I had with these folks helped clarify and bring back so many memories of the old days. Specifically: Jeff Lee, Dave Thiel, Howie Rubin, Matt Householder, Ron Waxman, Dennis Nordman, Rich Tracy, John Newcomer, Eugene Jarvis, George Petro, Larry DeMar, Chris Granner, Mark Loffredo, Jake Simpson, Ed Boon, John Tobias, Mark Turmell, Sal Divita, Steve Beran, Tony Goskie, John Vogel, Josh Tsui, Jim Weisz, and Todd Allen. I'm sure there are others I'm forgetting. My apologies.

Thanks must also go to so many more colleagues who I haven't seen of late, but were instrumental in the formation of the memories that made up my career, among them Jack Haeger, Ken Fedesna, Jun Yum, Kan Yabumoto, and so many more.

I'm grateful to the organizers of events who've been kind enough to invite me to come and share my stories: Doc Mack of Galloping Ghost Arcade outside Chicago; David Kaelin with the Classic Game Fest in Austin; Mike Stulir and Gary Vincent from ACAM (at Fun Spot in New Hampshire); Brandon Specht from Free Play Florida; Kalen Nelson with the Let's Play Expo outside Dallas; John Hardie, director of the National Videogame Museum in Frisco, Texas; Rob Berk with the Midwest Gaming Classic; Chuck Van Pelt from the Portland Retro Gaming Expo; and Dan and Holly Nikolich with the Rocky Mountain Pinball Showdown.

A number of friends agreed to read an early draft of the book and provide comments. I am forever grateful to Patrick Scott Patterson, Paul Drury, Tony Temple, James Kerwin, Brett Weiss, Genese Davis, and Van Burnham for their feedback.

General thanks go to other members of the retro-gaming community who are committed to seeing the history of video games preserved, game players whose skill at these older games is matched only by their love for them, and those involved with the International Video Game Hall of Fame who kindly honored me with an induction in 2018. My thanks go to Walter Day, Billy Mitchell, Paul Dean, Jerry Byrum, Bill Hoffman Jr., Ryan Burger, Todd Friedman, Michael Klug, Lonnie Macdonald, Jon Klinkel, and Julie Barwick, among many, many others.

I must also tip my hat to my friend, Josh Gates, whose memoir, *Destination Truth: Memoirs of a Monster Hunter*, inspired me to believe I might actually be able to write an entire book, too.

Of course, I thank my family for their eternal love and support.

And the final group of people I need to thank are the fans. Your interest and enthusiasm are the main reason I stepped back in time to preserve these stories. I genuinely enjoy meeting you, and I thank you for appreciating the work I did so many years ago.

I should reiterate that this book is filled with my personal recollections and perspectives, told as truthfully as possible. If there are any factual errors within, they are my sole responsibility.